EXCELLING IN SPORTS THROUGH THINKING STRAIGHT

THE AUTHORS

June E. Meyer is currently at William Fremd High School (Palatine, Illinois), chosen by the National Commission on Excellence in Education's National Secondary Schools Recognition Program as one of the top schools of 1987. She has been a Physical Education teacher for 24 years and has 15 years experience as a high school coach. A member of NASPSPA (North America Society of the Psychology of Sport and Physical Activity), Mrs. Meyer received a M.S. Degree in Communication from Governors State University (Illinois). She has lectured at clinics and has published articles concerning athletics and positive mental attitudes.

Carol A. Plodzien is a Physical Education teacher and Girls' Sports Coordinator at William Fremd High School (Palatine, Illinois), chosen one of the top schools of 1987 by the National Commission on Excellence in Education's National Secondary Schools Recognition Program. Having more than 15 years experience in coaching basketball at the high school level and compiling a lifetime record of 222-112, Ms. Plodzien's teams have won 50 consecutive games, six Conference Championships, six Regional Tournaments, one Sectional Tournament, one Super-Sectional Tournament, and finished in third place at the First Girls' State Tournament in Illinois. She was named Coach of the Year, 1983-84, and received the Women's Basketball Coaches Award, 1987. Ms. Plodzien is the current President of the Basketball Association for the Illinois Coaches Association for Girls' and Women's Sports. She has lectured extensively and published several articles in the field. She received her B.S. at Northern Illinois University and her M.S. at George Williams College.

EXCELLING IN SPORTS THROUGH THINKING STRAIGHT

The Right Choices for Players and Coaches

By

JUNE E. MEYER and **CAROL A. PLODZIEN**

Illustrations by
Roger Luteyn

With a foreword by
Coach Ray Meyer

CHARLES C THOMAS • PUBLISHER
Springfield • Illinois • U.S.A.

Published and Distributed Throughout the World by
CHARLES C THOMAS • PUBLISHER
2600 South First Street
Springfield, Illinois 62794-9265

This book is protected by copyright. No part of
it may be reproduced in any manner without
written permission from the publisher.

© *1988 by* CHARLES C THOMAS • PUBLISHER
ISBN 0-398-05474-6
Library of Congress Catalog Card Number: 88-3186

With THOMAS BOOKS *careful attention is given to all details of manufacturing and design. It is the Publisher's desire to present books that are satisfactory as to their physical qualities and artistic possibilities and appropriate for their particular use.* THOMAS BOOKS *will be true to those laws of quality that assure a good name and good will.*

Printed in the United States of America
Q-R-3

Library of Congress Cataloging in Publication Data

Meyer, June E.
    Excelling in sports through thinking straight: the right choice for players and coaches/by June E. Meyer and Carol A. Plodzien; illustrations by Roger Luteyn; with a foreword by Ray Meyer.
      p.   cm.
  Bibliography: p.
  Includes index.
  ISBN 0-398-05474-6
    1. Sports—Psychological aspects. 2. Achievement motivation. 3. Goal (Psychology) I. Plodzien, Carol A. II. Title.
GV706.4.M49   1988   88-3186
796'.01—dc19   CIP

*To all those we love,
so they can have it all!*

FOREWORD

THIS BOOK was written for athletes and coaches who want to be the best they can be. It is very educational and worthwhile. I learned a lot from Carol Plodzien and June Meyer. They set me thinking and they will do the same for you.

The thoughts and lessons you learn from this book can be applied to everyday life. You are the one who is responsible for what you are. You choose your own goals and how you go about obtaining them is entirely up to you. You are in control of your life. You have to focus on success and not on failures. A person must have confidence in his own ability and he can't be afraid to take risks to get what he wants. Too often I read of teams or players who played a game not to win but, rather, not to lose. If you don't have confidence in your own ability, why should anyone have confidence in you?

June and Carol have done an excellent job of portraying the correct thinking processes for athletes and coaches.

Coach Ray Meyer
DePaul Blue Demons, 1942 to 1984

PREFACE

THIS BOOK was written for athletes and coaches. The contents of the book allow athletes and coaches to see that they have choices that can lead them to be the best they can be.

We use a *whole brain* approach to athletics called *Thinking Straight*. *Thinking Straight* (T.S.) tells the athletes how to control the mind to enhance performance. Whole brain thinking allows you to blend physical and mental activity to reach your maximum potential. It helps you to gain control of your mind to develop self-discipline, responsibility, and to improve leadership and physical performance. T.S. *(Thinking Straight)* helps the athlete change doubtful thoughts to directed thoughts. It opens minds to new and different ideas. It increases energy levels for practices and games. T.S. also helps the athlete feel good about himself whether he's winning or losing. You can have complete control of your performance to a point where you are unaware of anything around you. T.S. helps you to be a whole brain thinker by controlling how you communicate, knowing you can achieve your goals, experiencing that working towards your goal is fun, taking the risk to go for what you want and, finally, experiencing the success that you created for yourself.

The book was written to show the athlete a step-by-step approach to identifying goals, thinking positively, being patient, and doing what is necessary to achieve the goal.

When you experience T.S., you can apply it to all parts of your life, not just athletics. And that's the real fun of it!

We want to say thank you to:

> Gloria Brandstat
> Geri Brongiel
> Pam Emmer
> Sue Guenther
> Dr. Audrey Klopp
> Joe Martina
> Christa Meyer
> Rob Meyer
> Suzi Meyer
> Marie Null
> Larry Petrillo
> Loralie Van Sluys
> Dr. William Thiel
> Joan Volberding

And a very special thank you to all of our athletes and students who were an important part in developing T.S., especially the Girls' Basketball Teams

INTRODUCTION: THINKING STRAIGHT—CHOOSING WHAT YOU WANT

OUR PHILOSOPHY is based on getting in touch with yourself, how you feel about yourself, and what you are saying to yourself. How can we love others if we don't love ourselves? We need to first experience loving ourselves before we can share it with others. It's just like when you are teaching your small child to cook. The experience of making cookies is much more successful, understandable, and more fun to the child if you have previously made the cookies and experienced the difficulties, techniques, and joy of making them first.

We believe you can have anything you want. What you do with your life and where you are right now is *your* choice. Sometimes we choose to do things for others or do what others want, telling ourselves that we are being used, when actually we have made the choice to be a loving, caring person. It is not what we have done that frustrates us, but what we are telling ourselves that creates our unhappiness. Other times we may choose to do things for ourselves or do what *we* want and tell ourselves that we are being selfish, which we denote as bad or negative. We have discovered that we do not have to look at situations in life as an either/or possibility. We can have what we want and also choose to do what others want. In the past, you may have thought you had to first give others what they wanted and then you could get what you wanted. Through experience we have found that after some people get what they want they usually go to their next want. Often we find that we expect other people then to give us what we want rather than for us to take responsibility for our own want. If we are committed to our own happiness and to what others want, we will be able to work out choices so we can find alternatives to get what we both want. It can be done if both people are willing to stay positive and committed to what they want.

Thinking Straight (T.S.) is a process that we have found helpful for finding out what it is we want and thinking positively toward that choice. T.S. provides a language for communicating positively with yourself and others. When you can express your feelings honestly and openly to others, it helps you to be a friend to yourself and to the other person. This can help you feel good about yourself. When you feel good about what you want, it's much easier to reach your goal. You will always attain that goal if it's what you really want.

In order to find out exactly what it is you want, we believe that *goal setting* and *risk taking* are essential. Goal setting gives you direction and helps you experience growth; it also helps you to stay positive about yourself and what you want. Focusing on your goals helps you to avoid obstacles. Risking helps you to overcome fears so you can attain your goal or get what you want. Many of us who choose to avoid risks stay in the same place. We give excuses as to why we don't want something or why someone won't give us what we want. Risking is vital and necessary to get what we want, as long as it is positive. By risking and focusing on yourself and what you want, you will experience *self-belief*. Believing in yourself means you can do whatever you want to do and that *you* have control over your life; this can help you overcome stress. None of this is possible unless you are willing to take responsibility to do the work of setting goals and risking to get what you want.

CONTENTS

                                                            Page

Foreword by Ray Meyer vii
Preface ix
Introduction: Thinking Straight — Choosing What You Want xiii

Chapter 1 Choices for Yourself 7
             Left Brain Functions 10
             Right Brain Functions 10
             Whole Brain Thinking 11
Chapter 2 You're a Real Character 17
             Which One Are You? 17
Chapter 3 Communication: T.S. Language 31
             The First Step to T.S. 31
             Negative T.S. Key Words 33
             Positive T.S. Key Words 36
Chapter 4 Goals: Finding Out What You Want 41
             The Second Step to T.S. 41
             Accepting What You Want 45
             Character Goals 47
             Committing to What You Want 51
Chapter 5 Work: Doing the Work 55
             The Third Step to T.S. 55
             Achieving Your Goal 56
Chapter 6 Risk: Conquering Your Fear of Failure 65
             The Fourth Step to T.S. 65
             Character Risks 71

Chapter 7 Growth: The Fun of It! 75
    Character Growths 75
    Personal Growths........................ 78
    Athletic Growths 81

References 85
Index 87

EXCELLING IN SPORTS THROUGH THINKING STRAIGHT

FEEL GOOD ABOUT YOUR CHOICE FOR YOURSELF!

HOW TO USE THIS BOOK

AT THE BEGINNING of each chapter, you will find statements or questions to help you start *Thinking Straight* (T.S.). These statements are designed to stimulate your thought processes and to help you relate to the information presented in the text of each chapter.

Also, starting with Chapter Three, the five steps of T.S. are outlined and can be used as building blocks to help you complete the specific T.S. steps. When linked together, each building block will assist you in reaching your goals and obtaining your maximum growth.

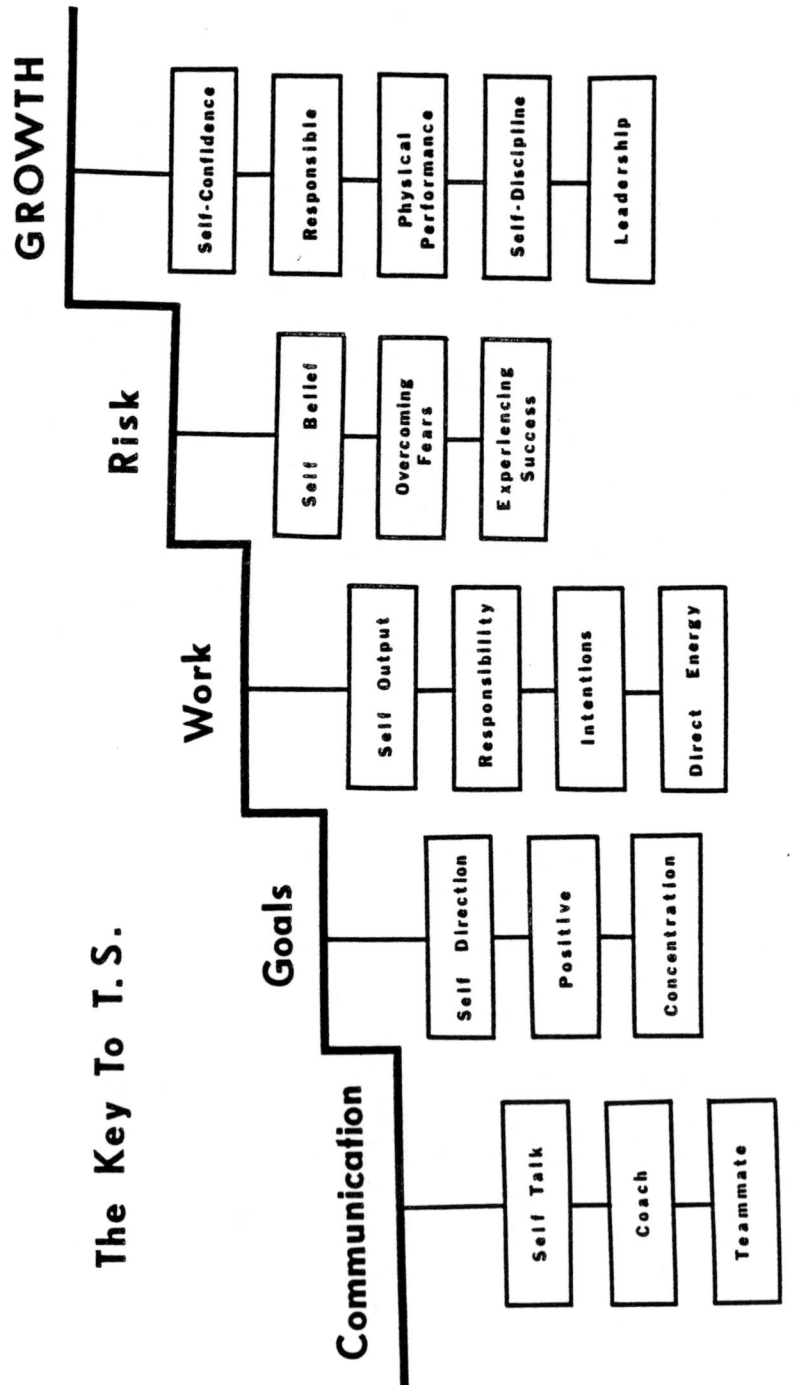

Figure 1. Key to T.S. Chart

CHAPTER 1

CHOICES FOR YOURSELF

IT IS OUR intention to share *Thinking Straight* with you so that you can start feeling better about yourself. *Thinking Straight* is a way to control yourself and to perform the way you want. The key of using T.S. is incorporating the following five steps into your life: communication, goals, work, risk, and experiencing your own growth. Here's how you can use these steps. T.S. gives you a specific language so you can communicate *positively* to yourself and others. Goal setting is essential because it gives you direction and helps you to achieve your goals and finally experience your successes. Setting goals is important because it helps you to stay positive about yourself and towards your goal. T.S. shows you how to use your self-output to do the work necessary to achieve your goal. It helps you to take 100 percent responsibility so you can direct all of your energy towards that goal. Risking helps you to overcome your fears and gives you self-belief so you can attain your goal. Risking is vital to experiencing T.S. because, without it, you will not be able to experience the fifth and final step: growth. By believing in yourself you can experience the success of achieving your goals. T.S. allows you to see the possibility of growth that is feasible for you. Some of the growth experiences you can have after using T.S. are: feeling self-confidence in whatever you are doing, improving your physical performance, and increasing your self-discipline. You will become a responsible person in whatever you are doing and discover that *you* can be a leader.

One of the most important concepts of T.S. is to realize that you do have choices about getting what you want out of your sport or out of any of life's situations which occur and in which we feel that we have no control. It is up to us to perceive these situations as either positive, which can be growth for us, or as negative, which can be destructive to us. Often, people don't realize that they do have choices, especially in situations that are important to them. For example, a softball coach usually picks twelve to fifteen players for the team. This year, because of the school's "no cut" rule, he is forced to keep all twenty-five players who are trying out for the team. Because the "no cut" rule is a decision that has already been made for the coach, he, like many other coaches, feels that he has no choice about how he wants to set up his softball program. But the coach really has one of four choices: to quit, to work with the better players, to divide his time equally among the players, or to develop a program that would motivate all players to maximize their best potential. It is important for the coach to realize that he does have choices and that he can get what he wants from his program.

Players have choices, too. For example, a highly-skilled swimmer wants to be on the team in the winter season and to also participate in a spring sport activity. The coach's requirements for being on the swim team are that all members must swim all year long, must attend morning and evening practices during the season, and may not be in any other activity or sport. The swimmer, because of the coach's requirements, feels that he has no choice except to swim year round if he wants to be a part of the swim team. If the swimmer accepts the coach's decision, he may become frustrated during the season because he is doing what someone else wants him to do and not what he would like to be doing. The swimmer does have choices. He can quit, which would make him feel bad about himself, because he wants to swim. His second choice would be to swim year round and realize and accept that he has made a positive choice for himself. However, if he really believes in his ability as a swimmer and wants to stay committed to what he wants (which is to swim on the team and participate in a spring activity), he can swim on the team, practicing mornings and evenings as the coach wants him to do. Then, in the spring during the off season, he can participate in the spring sport activity. When he returns to swim team practices in the fall or summer after doing what he wanted to do, he will be self-motivated to make the most out of his practices and swim his required times. The swimmer needs to realize that the coach may not want him back on the team. There is also a chance that the coach may keep him on the team because of his performance. Since the swimmer recognizes that he made the choice, he will be more positive toward practices and towards the coach and will give 100 percent effort to practice.

Just because a coach states what he wants does not mean that you can not have what you want. You must stay committed to what you want, listen to what the other person wants, and then look at all your options.

Stay committed to yourself and be positive toward your choice. Even though some people do not care about what you want or may not seem to care because they are so busy working toward what they want, continue to feel good about your choice and keep working toward that commitment.

We are sometimes hesitant to make a move unless we can be sure that this is the *right* move. Most of the time we continue to go through a situation following the same pattern, never considering the possibility that we could choose a different approach or look at the problem in a new way. Like the softball coach and the swimmer, our inability to choose gets us stuck between two alternatives, and we tell ourselves that we don't have any choices, or that our choices are limited. Usually when we make a choice, we want a guarantee that we have made the *correct* choice.

T.S. is a new approach for coaches and athletes. As coaches and teachers, we have found that many people are afraid or hesitant to do something new or different because they feel secure with their old way of doing things. At least they know how the old way will turn out. In his article *Communication: The Context of Change,* Dean C. Barnlunds states that:

> For most people, change is threatening. It is the old and familiar that is trusted, the novel and unknown that arouses alarm. To change is to give up cherished values, to be left defenseless and forced to assume responsibility for a new organization of experience.

Many times it seems scary to do something new and different because we don't realize that we have alternatives and we can't predict the outcome. We may say to ourselves that we are afraid of making a mistake or that we want to be sure to make the perfect choice. By doing things the old way we may be frustrated and miserable, but at least we will be comfortable and have a feeling of security. As John Dewey once said, "No one discovers a new world without forsaking an old one."

It is most important to select an immediate goal that you feel you want right now and then work toward that goal. No one can stop you but yourself. *YOU* are the one that sets limits on you, not others!

In order to grasp the concept of T.S. you will need to develop a new awareness of the human mind. Barbara Brown *(Super Mind)* refers to a new awareness of the subconscious mind by a large part of society. Society has become aware of the talents of the mind. These mind tools are surprisingly effective in achieving growth of the mind. A blend of physical and mental activity helps us to realize the dreams of our potential. We need to be aware of the unique resources of the mind. Sometimes we let groups or crowds change our thinking or behavior. Other times, when we are experiencing team momentum or group spirit, we can perform with abilities that we hardly knew were possible.

LEFT BRAIN FUNCTIONS

Much research has been devoted to the mind. Marilee Zdenek *(The Right Brain Experience)* discusses left and right brain hemispheres. The left brain deals with verbal, analytical, literal, linear, and mathematical functions, as well as physically controlling the right side of the body. The left brain is used to learn a skill or technique so that we can analyze or break it down and learn how to develop the skill. For example, when learning the lay-up shot in basketball, we first hear the coach's verbal description of the lay-up. We learn to analyze each movement, understand the linear motion of the pattern and break down the skill into each movement so that we can have total understanding of that skill.

Barbara Sherrod *(Illinois Career World Magazine),* in an article titled "Jobs for Right and Left Brainers," classifies the "left brainer" as someone who takes notes (lots of them), makes lists of things to do, finds out all they can about something new before starting on it, keeps talking until they make their point, and reads a financial report without crying.

RIGHT BRAIN FUNCTIONS

The right brain functions are nonverbal, holistic, spatial, musical, imaginative, artistic, sexual, spiritual, dream making, and controls the left side of the body. The right brain is the creative, intuitive and the "feeling" side of the brain. Rather than recall a specific skill and analyze each movement, the right brain is used to recall and FEEL learned movement patterns at random (as if you were on automatic pilot during performance or during a game situation). The body automatically flows from one movement to the next as if you were in a series of motion pictures doing everything correctly. For example, during a basketball game the player is aware of his spatial surroundings, has a feeling of being artistic and imaginative and has an instinctive feeling that he can make almost anything happen. In competitive athletics, the most visual effect of the right brain can be seen in one-on-one competition. When using right brain techniques, the athlete can narrow his focus of attention, eliminate outside distractions and concentrate on performance. He can combine both mental and physical energy into one controlled movement.

Barbara Sherrod's article states that people who are right brain dominant tend to have messy desks and will have friends who drop by without calling first. They are good at learning the latest dances, visualizing stories and ideas, and sensing trouble.

WHOLE BRAIN THINKING

The goal to T.S. is to develop a *whole brain* method of thinking. An effective person or player is one who combines caring, emotional support (right brain) with analytical knowledge of techniques and skills (left brain). An integration of emotional and analytical thinking results in a balance of whole brain thinking which enables one to focus clearly on goals, thus becoming the best player or person that one can possibly be. The whole brain method produces creative thinking and a more integrated person, one who is better able to motivate himself, to solve complex problems, to communicate and to tap all his inner resources.

There are two processes for whole brain thinking. The first process is left-to-right brain transfer of thoughts and the second process is right-to-left brain transfer. In left-to-right brain thinking, we create reality which releases our emotional reactions. For example, during a basketball game the coach needs a player who can accurately shoot from fifteen feet. When a player processes the coach's need using left-to-right brain thinking, he will try to recall each movement and perform the shot perfectly. This thinking works as long as the player makes the shot. He has *created* the emotional reaction of feeling good about himself and giving the coach what he wants. However, a conflict arises if the player misses the shot. On a missed shot, the player's left brain created reality will be, "I can't make the shot, and if I miss the shot the coach will take me out of the game." This left-to-right brain thinking creates a right brain emotional response of the player becoming upset and a feeling of letting the coach down or letting himself down. Now, instead of concentrating on the game or the techniques of shooting, the player is dwelling on his potential failure (the possibility of a missed shot). His emotional response continually magnifies the problem until the player won't shoot at all. In the second process of whole brain thinking, the right-to-left brain process, there is a sense of knowing that you can do something; this sense is confirmed in the left brain as *reality*. For example, during a game, the coach may tell the player he needs someone who can shoot from a range of fifteen feet. When the player processes the coach's need using right-to-left brain thinking, he has a sense of himself; he knows that he can do it. This thinking works because it combines the sense of knowing that you can do something (shooting) with the actual performance of the correct technique (the physical process of completing the shot).

During the basketball season, we experienced as coaches that it is possible to change left-brain-created reality to right-brain-thinking reality. One of the guards at the regional tournament basketball game was practicing her shot in the pregame warmup period. She starting missing a few shots and, as she continued to miss, she became tense and worried that she was not going to be able to shoot during the game. She ran over to the coach and asked her to watch her shot to see what she was doing wrong. As the coach watched, the guard kept shooting and missing. The guard was correcting one technique only to find that she was creating other problems. Nothing seemed to help her and she became increasingly frustrated. Finally, she decided that maybe she was just not able to shoot on that particular day and nothing the coach could say would change her thinking. We asked her to stop thinking about *how* to shoot and to think about what she knew intuitively. Did she know if she could shoot correctly? Did she know the proper technique for shooting? If she could get in touch with knowing that she really did know how to shoot correctly, she would be able to concentrate on her shot and feel confident instead of fearful. As soon as she started thinking positively and was committed to her ability, her thinking was switched to a *sense* of knowing (right brain) and she was able to perform at her true ability level in the regional game.

In Figure 2 the player *can shoot* because he is thinking right-to-left; he *can't shoot* when he is thinking left-to-right. Whole brain thinking allows the player, by using his right brain, to feel good about himself and gives him a sense of knowing and tapping his left brain for use of specific learned materials or techniques.

T.S. can teach you how to use the whole brain method of thinking. The ultimate goal of T.S. is to use the process to become a whole brain person. It can help you experience complete control of your performance in any situation or game to a point where you are unaware of anything around you (crowd, referees, parents, peers, or opponents). T.S. is a process by which you can get in touch with the positive reality which already exists within yourself. By using the five steps of T.S., you can be a whole brain thinker by controlling how you communicate;

Figure 2. How are you thinking, left or right brain?

knowing you can achieve your goal; experiencing working toward your goal as fun; taking the risk to go for what you want, and finally experiencing the success that you created for yourself.

Why use the whole brain method of thinking? So that you can be the best person that you can be whether you are in athletics, working at your job or in relationships with other people. To be effective, the coach needs to be creative (right brain) for practices and game situations and also needs to be able to give clear directions (left brain) to the athletes for organized practice sessions. The athlete, taking a step-by-step breakdown of each skill performed (left brain), also needs to create and imagine movements (right brain) for practice and game situations. By meeting the challenge of whole brain thinking, you will be able to create success for yourself.

HOW DO YOU **SEE** YOURSELF?

CHAPTER 2

YOU'RE A REAL CHARACTER

HOW MANY TIMES have you had low self esteem and put yourself down around other people saying things like, "I could never learn how to do that," or "I could never do that as well as he does"? Have you heard other people say, "It's not my fault," or "I have to get this perfect," or "It won't be good enough"?

After observing and working with a large number of students, athletes and coaches, we have discovered that there are eight different *Thinking Straight* characters. We have given them names so that you can easily identify with them.

By understanding these distinct personalities, you can better understand yourself and others. The T.S. characters were developed out of a process of helping students, athletes, friends, and professional colleagues reach their goals. Most often, because of your behavior patterns, you will consistently be identified with one character type. That character and behavior type usually involves a situation which is most important to you. In different situations you may find yourself assuming another character type. In some situations you could be a combination of characters.

WHICH ONE ARE YOU?

Paul Putdown. Usually puts himself down by comparing himself with others and never feels that he is good enough or as good as the other person.

Melissa Mistake. Usually worries about making a mistake. She is so focused on mistakes that she creates them.

David Dolittle. Wants to be successful, but doesn't do the work. He thinks that he knows it all and is not willing to listen or to learn.

Patty Perfect. Feels she has to do everything perfectly before she can experience success in her sport or activity.

Rita Rescue. Is so concerned about helping everyone else that she often forgets to consider herself and work on the skills that she needs.

Willy Worry. Is constantly worrying about everything and everyone else. He will focus on what has happened in the past or worries about what might happen in the future. He rarely experiences the moment.

Brenda Blame. Fails to take responsibility for her failures or credit for her successes.

Eddie Ego. Has superior knowledge and ability in his field and is a constant threat to those who work with him. Eddie doesn't have the immediate problem; the others have a problem with Eddie. Eddie is centered on himself.

Figure 3. Paul Putdown (Before T.S.)

Paul Putdown

Paul feels inadequate in his abilities and doubts that he can achieve what he wants. Because he lacks self-confidence and self-esteem, he is continually saying to himself, "He is better than me." To Paul, the other person is always better than he is.

For example, during warm-ups for the 100 meter dash, Paul notices other runners and what they are doing. He constantly compares their warm-up and body builds to himself. He says negative things to himself like, "Look how flexible he is," and "His legs look stronger than mine. He has the best qualifying time in the area. I can't beat him."

Instead of focusing his thoughts on the other runner, Paul needs to focus on his strengths and to gain self-confidence. Just because the other runner's legs look stronger does not mean that they *are* stronger.

Figure 4. Paul Putdown (After T.S.)

Melissa Mistake

Melissa usually worries about making a mistake instead of thinking about what she does well or how good she feels. She's afraid things won't work out right and she won't get what she wants or deserves. By focusing on her fears, she actually creates a mistake. Her fear stops her from getting what she wants.

Figure 5. Melissa Mistake

For example, Melissa is a varsity tennis player. She advances to the first doubles position for the conference meet. She has previously played at the second doubles position for regular conference meets. Because she is playing in the first doubles position, Melissa feels that she needs to play better than she did as a second doubles player and should make fewer mistakes on her serves. She begins to think of things like, "Will I get the ball in the service court? What if I foot fault? Will I hit the net?"

Melissa needs to focus on her intentions of how she wants to perform during the meet. She needs to visualize herself performing each movement or skill correctly and to the best of her ability.

David Dolittle

David wants to be successful but doesn't want to do the work. He just goes through the motions of doing the work and never really changes anything. He stays with his old habits and remains stagnant in his skills. In reality, he doesn't believe that doing the work will get him what he wants. He believes there is only one way to do something, and his mind is not open to new or different ideas.

For example, David was the high scorer on the junior varsity basketball team. This year David is moved up to the varsity level. His scoring average drops considerably. The coach shows David a new shooting technique that would improve his average, but it would take time to

Figure 6. David Dolittle

work on the shooting drills to achieve this skill. The coach knows that progressing to higher levels of competition would require increasing skill level. David begins saying to himself, "Why does the coach want me to change? This is the way I shoot. I've had success before. I can't change now! I'll do the drills, but it's not going to do any good."

If David really wants to be successful, he needs to be open to new ideas and give them a chance instead of staying with his old habits.

Patty Perfect

Patty feels that she has to be perfect in anything she does. If she cannot perform the way she expects, she feels that she is not good enough for the team. She often feels that she has not only let herself down, but that she has let the team down as well. She is usually resistant and inflexible to different or new ideas. She lacks self-encouragement and doesn't accept herself as

Figure 7. Patty Perfect

being okay the way she is. Because of her obsession to get everything right, she forgets that she has other options or choices.

For example, Patty is a forward on the varsity basketball team. In her own mind, in order for her to play a good game, she has to score a certain amount of points when she goes into the game. Feeling this way when she enters the game, she might say to herself, "I can't miss my shot," or "I have to make this shot." Patty feels that if she takes the place of another player on the court and misses the shot, then her teammates and coach will not think she is good enough to play. Often she thinks that others can do a better job than she can. She might even think that she will let the coach down or lose the game for the team.

Patty needs to forget about what other people think and just concentrate on her shot or herself. She needs to realize that no one is perfect and that everyone makes a mistake once in awhile. She needs to concentrate more on encouraging herself and having confidence in her shot. By giving herself a pat on the back, she will begin to feel comfortable on the court and begin to look for options and choices for shooting. She will then experience success.

Rita Rescue

Rita is so concerned about helping everyone else that she often forgets herself. She is often undecided about what she wants to do and

Figure 8. Rita Rescue

doesn't set priorities that include herself. Because she tries to do things for other people, her behavior is based on other peoples' needs rather than her own. If she does decide what she wants to do, she often does it either with an aggressive manner by fighting for her rights or in a passive manner by keeping what she wants to herself and hoping others will give it to her.

For example, Rita is a forward on the girls' soccer team. During practice, the coach gives the team time to work on any individual skills that they want to work on. Rita wants to work on her ballhandling. A teammate asks Rita if she would help her work on passing. Because Rita can't say "no" to anyone, she will agree to help her teammate and give up what she wants to do. She usually responds by saying, "Sure, I'll help you." As Rita is working with the teammate, she becomes impatient because she is thinking about what she wants to do and gets irritated at her teammate. The coach blows the whistle to signal one minute left of practice. Rita, very disgusted, says to herself, "Oh no; time's up already and I didn't even get a chance to work on my ballhandling!"

The same situation will occur practice after practice until Rita becomes frustrated enough to finally give herself time to work on the specific skills that she wants to work on. Rita knows what she wants to do; she just needs to tell her teammates and then they can help each other to set priorities so they can all accomplish what they want to do. By communicating with her teammates and setting priorities, Rita can stay committed to what she would like to do (ballhandling) and still have time to help her teammates, which always makes her feel good about herself.

Willy Worry

Willy is continuously worrying about anything and everything. He tends to focus on the past or future situations rather than on the present. He doesn't feel that he has control over any situation involving himself. Because he thinks that he has little or no control over himself or situations, he often feels threatened, frustrated, or angry. Willy believes others are in control of him and that he has little power over situations in which he is involved.

For example, Willy is a senior who is a receiver on the varsity football team. During his junior year, he was a successful, outstanding receiver. Now Willy is beginning to drop every pass that is thrown to him during the games. He is worried about why he can't catch the ball. Looking back at his junior year, Willy begins to think, "Gosh, I rarely missed a pass last year. Now it seems as if I don't have enough time to catch the ball." Willy is becoming frustrated and feels threatened that the coach will take his starting position away. He is not only worried about football, he is also worried about getting his homework finished, making high grades so he can get a scholarship and go to the college that he wants and being able to succeed in his future career. Willy is feeling everything is out of his control and that everything he does is something he *has* to do.

Willy needs to direct all his energy toward one goal at a time. He needs to focus on what he is doing at the present. He can still have his long range plans, but his immediate focus should be on the moment. By

Figure 9. Willy Worry

focusing on what he wants now, he will be able to efficiently plan his time, get more accomplished, and enjoy what he is doing right now. He will find that he seems to have all the time in the world to catch those passes while he still enjoys everything at the moment.

Brenda Blame

Brenda fails to take responsibility for her failures or credit for her successes. Brenda feels that what others do has a direct effect on her. Because she depends on other people, she feels they often let her down, especially in situations which are important to her. Brenda also projects her own guilt on other people. If things do not turn out the way Brenda thinks they should, she often blames others so that she can be right.

For example, Brenda is on the junior varsity gymnastics team. At practice Brenda and her teammates watch a varsity gymnast practice her routine on the uneven parallel bars. Brenda turns to her friend and says, "We'll never be that good because the varsity coach won't spend any time with us." Brenda wants to be on the varsity team and does not

Figure 10. Brenda Blame

want to take the responsibility to get the help she needs, so she blames the coach. She feels it's the coach's fault that she is not on the varsity team because he doesn't spend time with her. Because gymnastics is important to her, she tends to blame others and feels that they have let her down or won't help her to improve her skills.

Brenda needs to take responsibility and do what is necessary to improve her skills so she can achieve what she wants in gymnastics. She needs to stop blaming other people and start believing in herself. When she feels that she is important enough to ask the varsity coach for help, she will then be ready to perform as a varsity gymnast.

Eddie Ego

Eddie has superior knowledge and ability in his field and is a constant threat to others who work with him. He is independent; knows what he wants to do as well as what needs to be done; likes to take risks; is creative, self-confident, self-centered; has self-discipline and a high level of physical performance; displays leadership qualities, and knows his positive strengths. Eddie Ego does not have a problem because he always takes responsibility for what he wants to do. Often he will have suggestions on how the group can work more effectively together. Usually any problems that may develop with Eddie stem from the people who work with him. These people may feel threatened by Eddie's superior knowledge and ability and, as a result, they become one of the previous seven characters.

For example, Eddie is an outstanding guard on the varsity basketball team. During a time-out in the game, Eddie makes a suggestion to the coach about what strategy the team needs to be using to be more effective on their offense. After Eddie's suggestion, the coach begins to feel threatened, even though he knows Eddie is right. He says to himself, "Players should not coach the game. I'm the coach, and I'm in charge of the game plan." Now, the coach becomes a Patty Perfect and tells Eddie during the time out, "No, we are staying with what I say." Eddie says, "But, coach, it will work." And the coach says, "*I am the coach; I will make the decisions.*" Eddie's teammates are now frustrated because the time-out was wasted between Eddie and the coach. Now they do not have any directions for their game plan. They become a "Brenda Blame" and start blaming Eddie for wasting their time-out. Eddie's mother and father become a Willy Worry because they are concerned about the other players' reactions towards Eddie. They find it difficult to under-

Figure 11. Eddie Ego

stand why a person with Eddie's knowledge and ability cannot relate well with the other players or the coach. They also become Brenda Blame by blaming others (the coach and Eddie's teammates) for Eddie's unhappiness and try to become Rita Rescue by trying to fix the situation.

Eddie often will start to believe what others are saying. He sometimes becomes concerned, not understanding what he is doing that makes everyone so upset, and begins to focus on what the other players are saying instead of on his skills.

Eddie needs to continue to be himself and go for what he wants by focusing on his physical performance or skills and to remain open-minded. He needs to understand that even though he may be right, other people will have their beliefs and opinions and there is little he can do to change them. Regardless of how others react, he needs to remain enthusiastic and keep his self-esteem.

Now that you are familiar with our eight characters, how many times have you experienced being with a Paul Putdown, Melissa Mistake,

David Dolittle, Patty Perfect, Rita Rescue, Willy Worry, Brenda Blame, or Eddie Ego? Knowing and understanding these characters and what they are thinking can help you to understand your own behavior as well as others. Our behavior is an outward display of how we feel about ourselves. Now that you are beginning to understand the behavior patterns of the characters, you will know why each one acts the way he does. The *Thinking Straight* characters can be found in any life situation, not just athletics.

IMPROVE YOUR COMMUNICATION

DO YOU HAVE CONTROL OVER YOU?

Communication

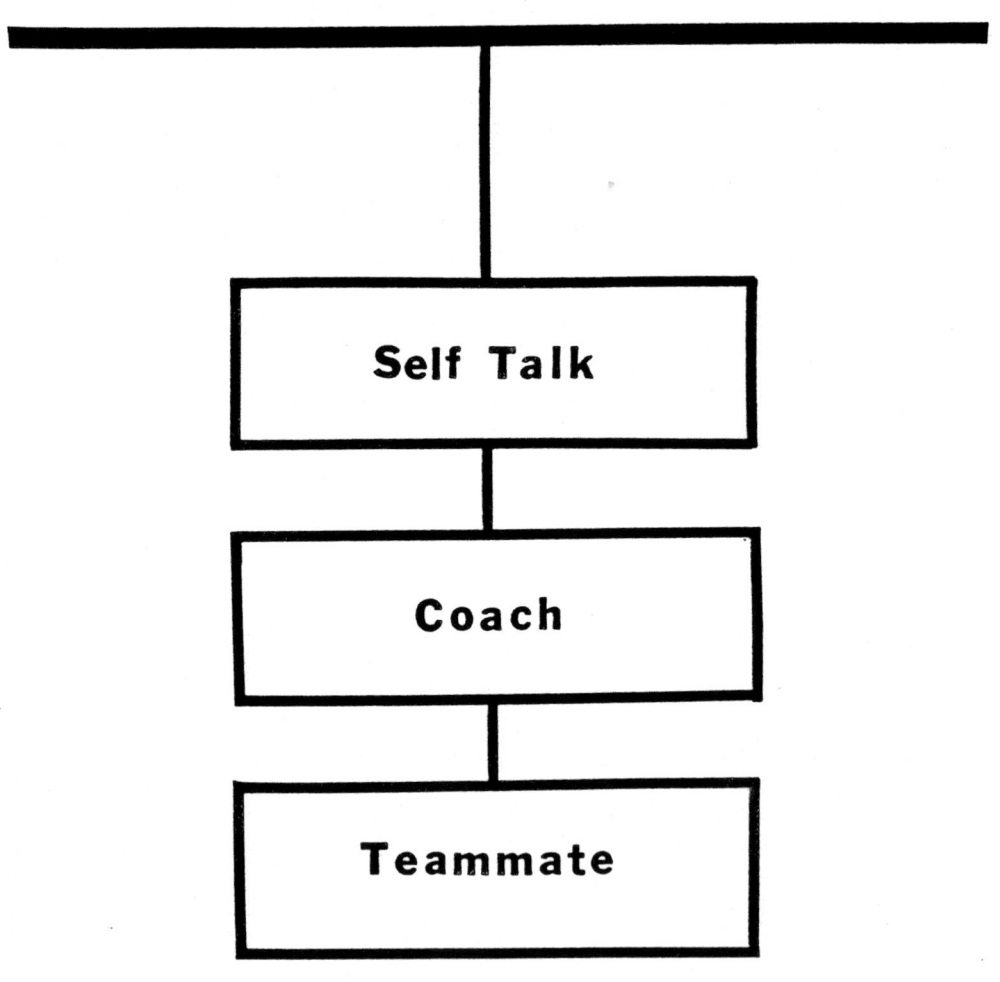

CHAPTER 3

COMMUNICATION: T.S. LANGUAGE

THE FIRST STEP TO T.S.

MANY TIMES what people say and what they mean are two different things. You need to condition yourself to be aware of the messages that you are saying to yourself and what you are verbalizing to others.

Are you aware of your *self-talk?* We are continually talking to ourselves with silent thoughts. Our minds are constantly sending and repeating thoughts which can be either on a conscious or an unconscious level. By using T.S. you can learn to listen to your self-talk, analyze what you are really thinking and understand that you do have control over how you feel and think. Do you really analyze your self-talk? Most people don't! By learning to listen to your self-talk you can better understand why you are saying certain thoughts to yourself. Are these thoughts a correct understanding of the situation and are you saying what you really want to be saying? When listening to yourself and what others are saying, you can hear what is really being said. If you are not in touch with what you are thinking, it is difficult to express what you want.

Messages can be either positive or negative words or statements. When you are feeling happy and good about yourself, you are sending positive messages such as, "I'm feeling awesome today," "Today is a great day," or "This is fun!" When you are unhappy or not feeling good about yourself, your negative messages may sound like: "I'm tired," "What a crummy day," or "Why me?" A lot of times, you are not aware that you are saying things to yourself. Some people have thoughts in their heads and others actually hear a little whiney voice that communicates to them.

When things become important, you can be saying up to 800 words per minute to yourself. And since the situation is something important, the voice is usually rapidly repeating thoughts that are NEGATIVE, especially if you are not confident of your abilities. Over a period of years, if you continue to listen to that voice, you will become conditioned to what it is saying and you will start *believing* what is being said. You will become unhappy and begin to feel bad about yourself. When you are feeling negative about yourself, you won't even hear the POSITIVE thoughts or statements, you will only focus on the negative ones. In any situation, the positive and negative thoughts both exist. Depending on how you feel about yourself, you will focus on one or the other. For example, a teenager daughter comes home from school, and the mother calmly says, "Hi! You're home; what took you so long?" The daughter, thinking negatively about herself, snaps back at her mother saying, "So, I can't help it! You didn't say I had to be home at a certain time!" If the daughter was feeling good about herself or confident that what she did was okay, she would hear her mother's statement as positive and realize that her mother was just concerned about her safety or might just be glad to see her. If the daughter was thinking positively, her response might explain the reason she was late and she might want to talk to her mother: "Hi. I want to tell you what we did after school. It was really fun!"

A similar situation could occur during an athletic event where the player hears the coach's response as either a positive or negative statement. For example, on the day of a practice the coach is preoccupied with situations involving students, colleagues, and phone calls. A player passing the coach in the hallway says, "Hi!" With other things on his mind, the coach does not hear the player and gives no response. If the player was feeling good about himself, he would consider the possibility that the coach didn't hear him. When thinking negatively, the player would assume that the coach was mad at him or in a bad mood. The player could accept his negative choice and dwell on it until it affects him at practice. Or he could choose to not be affected by the coach's lack of response and have a great practice, performing to the best of his ability. Steven J. Danish and Bruce K. Hale, *Teaching Psychological Skills to Athletes and Coaches,* refer to self-talk statements that athletes make to themselves. Statements that the athletes make about their abilities often become beliefs which limit their performance. The athlete is so busy criticizing himself and thinking negative thoughts that he concentrates on his mistakes rather than on what he needs to do to correct his performance. The athlete needs to concentrate on his specific skills in the game to improve his performance.

Listen to your self-talk and be aware of what you are really saying and thinking. As Shakespeare once said, "There is no good or bad, it's just our thinking that makes it so."

How do you know when you are thinking positively or negatively? T.S. indicates positive or negative thinking by focusing on the T.S. KEY WORDS. By focusing on these words you can get in touch with what you are saying or how you are thinking.

NEGATIVE T.S. KEY WORDS

| CAN'T | SHOULD | WISH | BUT | HAVE TO |
| TRY | MUST | HOPE | SORRY | MAYBE |

How do you know these words are negative? Let's look at how they are used in real life or athletic situations?

Can't

When you say, "*I can't,*" what you are really saying is, "*I won't.*" It may be possible for you to perform a certain task and, for some reason, you are choosing not to do it. It may be a good reason or it may only be an excuse. Like the softball coach earlier who said, "*I can't* run a softball program with the 'no cut' rule," he is choosing to think that his program can only be successful one way. Or, like a student who *can't* get all his homework finished for math class. He is choosing to do other things and *won't* finish his homework. Although the math student has other alternatives for getting his homework finished, he still chooses to say he *can't*.

Sports-Related Example of the Word *Can't*

An athlete might use the word *can't* as follows: "Coach, I *can't* shoot free throws this way." What the player is really saying is, "I *won't* shoot free throws the coach's way; I want to do it my way."

Should — Have To — Must

When using *should*, you feel that you have to do what the other people tell you to do. You feel obligated to do what others want, instead of what you want to do. With peer pressure you encounter many *shoulds*. Let's say a teenager wants to stay home and relax or just do her own thing. Her friend wants her to go to a party with her. She is telling herself, "I *should* go to the party with my friend because if I don't go, my friend will feel bad if she doesn't have anyone to go with to the party." Now if she does go she may have a terrible time, because she didn't stay at home and relax as she had originally planned.

Sports-Related Example of the Word *Should*

A soccer player might say, "The coach told me I *should* practice my dribbling and passing." If the soccer player does not feel it's his choice, he will not be as enthusiastic in his practice and it will be a waste of his time.

Wish — Hope — Maybe

When using the words *wish*, *hope*, and *maybe*, you have no intention of doing whatever you said you were going to do. You already know it's not going to happen because you have put the control of the situation outside of yourself. A student near failing says, "I *hope* I pass my history test; I didn't even study." The student already knows he is either going to do poorly or fail the test. He has no intention of passing the test or he would have studied. He falsely believes the control of his grade is now in the teacher's hands rather than his.

Sports-Related Example of the Word *Hope*

A badminton player might say, "I *hope* I win this match." She is not sure of herself and, instead of making it her intention to play her best and concentrate on the game and how she is playing, she is putting the results of the game to chance. She feels she has little control of the situation.

Sorry

When you use the word *sorry*, it is often an excuse so you don't have to do something. When you do what YOU want instead of what someone else wants you to do, you use the word *sorry* as an excuse so you won't feel bad about yourself. A mother says to her daughter, "You forgot to wash the dishes again. Get in here and do them right now!" The daughter responds saying, "*Sorry*, Mom, I forgot. I was doing my homework." Doing the dishes is the mother's idea; the daughter uses the word *sorry* as an excuse so she will not feel bad about not doing what her mother wants her to do. Many times *sorry* is used as an apology to make ourselves and others feel better. This is an accepted use of the word.

Sports-Related Example of the Word *Sorry*

A setter on the volleyball team might say to her teammate who wants to spike the ball, "*Sorry,* I passed to Jamie instead of you." The setter doesn't want to pass to her teammate.

But

Anytime you use the word *but* you are canceling out the first part of your statement. For example, a student says, "I want to go see the game tonight, *but* my mom won't let me." In the first part of her statement the student states what she thinks she wants, "I want to go see the game tonight." In the second part of her statement, "Mom won't let me," the student is blaming her mother for not allowing her to do what she thinks she wants to do. What the student is really saying is that she does not want to go to the game and uses her mother as an excuse for not going.

Sports-Related Example of the Word *But*

A player says to the coach, "I know that's the way you want me to do it, *but* it doesn't work for me. It works better to do it this way." The player does not want to do it the coach's way. She only wants her own way, so she invents the excuse that the coach's way won't work.

Try

When you *try* you are only attempting to get what you think you want. You can *try* to do something many times, and until you decide to do it, it's not going to happen. The reason we *try* is because we don't believe we can do whatever it is we want or because it's not something we really want to do. For example, a student says, "I *tried* to finish my homework, but there are too many interruptions at home." As long as the student remains in the same environment, he has no intention of getting his homework done. If the student really wants to get his homework done, he will take responsibility and find a place where there are no interruptions.

Sports-Related Example of the Word *Try*

During a softball game, the coach tells the shortstop, "Come on, we need a hit!" The player says, "I'll *try.*" Since the player doesn't believe he can get a hit, he will only make an attempt to hit the ball.

When you hear yourself using these key words, you can alert your conscious mind that you are thinking negative thoughts. These words only serve as excuses for not achieving your goals.

By improving your communication to yourself and to others, you can have control over yourself. In order to change your negative thoughts to positive thoughts, you need to be aware of the T.S. POSITIVE KEY WORDS.

POSITIVE T.S. KEY WORDS

WANT   CAN   WILL

By changing your negative words to positive words, you are focusing your energy on something that you want to do, not on something that you don't want to do. By changing your verbal patterns to positive words, you are connecting to the right brain thinking which enables you to use a whole brain thought process. This changes negative thinking to positive thinking. When you are focused positively on what you want, you begin to see all the choices available to you. Then you are willing to do everything it takes to achieve what you want. One example relates to the math student who couldn't get his homework done for class. By focusing his thoughts on the T.S. positive words and determining what he *wants* to do, he will be able to see other available choices. He will be able to organize his time better so that he can do his homework and the other things that he enjoys. He says, "I *want* to do my homework, and I *can*, if I organize my time."

An athlete says, "*Sorry* coach, *but* I *can't* get to my offensive position, because the other team is set up in a different defense." The player is not making it his intention to get to a position to make the offensive game play work. When you use *sorry* and *but*, you only make excuses for yourself. To change to a positive, the player says, "I *will* get into position to make this offense work, no matter what it takes or how the defense is set up. We practiced how to fake to the left so I can get my opponent out of position, and I know I *can* do it."

Or an athlete might think, "I *should* practice my passing because the coach said I need more work on accurate passes." To change to positive, he says, "I *want* to practice my passing, and I *will* improve." He then begins to see some of the choices that are available to him because he is thinking positively about what he wants to do, and he will remember, "The drills I learned in practice last night are just what I need."

Sports Dialogues

The first step to T.S. is communication. Here are three sports related dialogues between players and coaches that point out how important this new language is to communication.

Football

A player says to himself before the game: "Mom, Dad, and Grandma are coming to the game tonight. I *have to* play well and I *can't* make any mistakes. I want them to be proud of me."

During the game the player says to himself: "Oh no, that was a dumb pass. I knew he would intercept it! Next time I'll *try* to throw it higher."

The next time he throws the ball in the game: "Oh no, too high. I *have to* get the pass right; the coach is yelling at me. I *can't* make any more mistakes."

Next time: "Oh no! Another bad pass. It looked like he was open."

The player thinks to himself on the bench: "Why *can't* I do anything right? What will Mom and Dad think?"

The coach asks the player: "What are you thinking?"

Player: "I don't know, I'm *sorry, but* I just *can't* pass."

The coach, realizing the statement is negative, helps the player think positively by stating, "You know you *can* pass. Why do you think that you can't pass tonight?"

Player: "My defender is right on top of me and I don't have time to pass."

Coach: "Then you need to use alternatives (choices). What about the fakes you learned in practice this week?"

Player: "Yeah, I forgot about those. I *can* do it!"

Player says to self later in the game: "That felt great! I *can* pass like this all night!"

Basketball Practice

Player to coach: "I'm frustrated. My new shot isn't working. I just *can't* shoot this way. I'm *trying* to do it right! Can't I go back to my old shot?"

Coach: "Listen to the negative words you are saying to yourself. *CAN'T! TRY!* Your language indicates that you don't want to use your new shot or you don't believe you will have success with the new shot."

Player: "I do want to use the new shot."

Coach: "Why? Because I want you to, or because you want to? If you are doing it for me, then the shot won't be successful. You need to use the new shot because you want to."

Player: "I want to, *but* there are so many things to remember."

Coach: "If you really *want* to use the new shot, then you need to think positively, know that you *can* shoot the new way, be patient and take it one step at a time."

Volleyball Practice

Player #1 the day before the game: "This offense is too hard. There are too many options, and I *can't* remember where to go. I *hope* I can do it right in the game."

T.S. Player #2: "Wow! Are you negative. What do you mean you can't do the offense? You *won't*! You are only *trying*."

Player #1: "What do you mean I'm *trying?*"

T.S. Player #2: "*Trying* is only attempting to do the offense. Did you review the handout or talk to the coach?"

Player #1: " Yes, I *tried,* but the coach was busy."

T.S. Player #2: "If you want to understand the offense, then you need to talk to the coach."

T.S. Player #2 after the game: "Hey, you did a good job on offense tonight."

Player #1: "Thanks. You helped me realize that I was thinking negatively. Talking to the coach helped me to think positively and showed me what I needed to do to run the offense. I feel great."

Listening to your *self-talk* will help you to improve communication to yourself, to the coach, to your teammates and to others in a positive way. By using this new T.S. language, you can focus on what you want.

MAKE YOUR WANTS
POSITIVE!

Goals

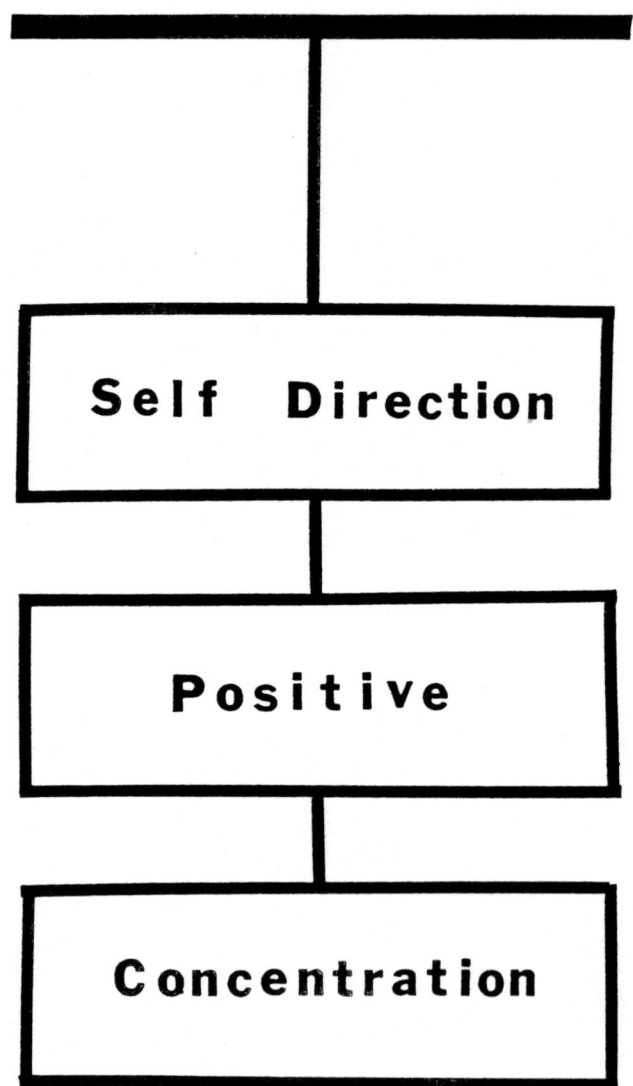

CHAPTER 4

GOALS: FINDING OUT WHAT YOU WANT

THE SECOND STEP TO T.S.

MOST PROBLEMS stem from either not knowing what you want or not communicating what you want. You need to be clear of your goal because you can often waste a lot of energy either seeking things you really don't want or moving around without purpose. Often you are telling yourself that you want some other goal more or that the goal you are pursuing is not the one you want. If you *do* know what you want, it is often hard to communicate to others in a clear, assertive way exactly what it is that you want. You either stop communicating altogether, telling yourself the person already knows what you want, or you tell someone in a very aggressive, angry manner what you want and expect them to give it to you. For example, an athlete will say he can't (won't) tell the coach or other players how he feels about certain situations involving the team, the game, the coach, or personal goals. It is difficult to communicate something that is very important to you. Because of the athlete's lack of communication, he becomes frustrated and many times cannot play to his potential. His frustration stems from either not getting what he thinks he wants or not knowing exactly what it is he wants. Remember at this time and place that you ALWAYS GET WHAT YOU WANT! At any given moment the choice of what you want is really yours. You really have chosen to be frustrated about your situation, which means going along with the situation and making yourself unhappy. And sometimes you may choose to change the situation by giving yourself what you want. Sometimes you may choose to remove yourself from the situation, which will give you temporary relief. However, the situation will need to be dealt with sometime in your life, now or later. Many times we disagree that we have what we want, especially if we are frustrated or angry about something. We also tend to be more concerned about what other people want. We are very good at seeing what others want and tend to make our wants secondary. This is especially true if it involves someone who is important to us or occurs in a situation that we consider vital to our happiness. Instead of seeing our want or goal as a possibility, we refuse to believe that we can have it or believe that we have a choice. If you set your mind on something positive with direction or goals, you will always be able to attain it. Sometimes we would rather focus on the lack of something or on the frustration rather than believe the attainability of it and strive for what we want. Once you have considered what you want and taken action towards it, you will be able to consider others' goals. This is very important when working with a team.

How do you know what you want? A want is a desire to obtain something for yourself. You all have the answer within yourself; you know what it is that you want. Sometimes you may be just afraid to admit it or to see it because you think you can't have it. When deciding what you want, there are TWO RULES that you need to follow:

RULE #1: MAKE YOUR WANTS OR GOALS ABOUT YOURSELF.

RULE #2: MAKE YOUR WANTS OR GOALS POSITIVE.

When deciding what you want, be specific and center that goal or want around yourself. You do not have control over another person. You do have control over yourself. It may seem difficult to make your wants about yourself at first. Most of us have a tendency to make our wants about someone else. We want them to give us something or to behave in a certain manner, or we want them to do things in a particular way. As long as you believe that you can control what others think or do, you can cause yourself much frustration. You need to stay centered on yourself and your goals. In the past, you may have been taught to do what others want you to do. You may feel it's not okay to do what you want. By constantly doing what others want you to do, you may start to expect that they will give you what you want in return. Unfortunately, it doesn't always work out that way, and you soon begin to become frustrated with the waiting. You may begin to feel that they don't care about what you want. Actually, *you* don't care what you want when you're with them. As long as you continue to work towards other peoples' wants or goals, you will find it difficult or nearly impossible to work for what you want. You will find that you are paying more attention to their goals than to your own.

An example of making your wants or goals about others in an athletic situation would be: As a guard on the basketball team, you have a goal of starting each game. Playing in the game is important, but being able to start the game is most important to you. You want the coach to put you into the game as a starter. You are now making your want or goal about the coach. You are giving the coach control over your goal. If he decides he wants you in the game, you reach your goal. If he decides he wants someone else in the game, you will not reach your goal. The coach may have other ideas, goals, or wants. If you continue to allow the coach to have control over your goals or wants, you will become frustrated because you cannot control another person. You do have control over yourself. If your want or goal is to start, then you need to modify your behavior very specifically in order to attain the goal for that sport or situation. You need to find out from the coach what talents and skills a starter on his team would need to perform. Now you will know what to work on to get that starting position. You can then set goals for yourself. You need to concentrate on each goal or skill and work on them one at a time in practice. Always work on being the best that you can be. You need to make a list of what you want out of your sport. What long-range goals would you like to accomplish? What are your short-range goals? What kinds of goals would be best for everyday practices or games? For example, in basketball, maybe you want to be the player on the team with the most assists, highest scoring average, best free throw percentage. Perhaps you would like to be an all conference player, or be selected as an all state player. You could concentrate on some of these goals and work towards them. They can be realistic goals for anyone.

Here are some specific examples of wants or goals for yourself. As a player you want to improve your individual statistics in:

1. Improving basic fundamental skills.
2. Improving form or technique.
3. Completing passes.
4. Increasing speed.
5. Shooting more to improve scoring average.
6. Making more assists.
7. Improving batting average.
8. Improving free throw percentage.

As soon as you have selected very specific goals for yourself, then you can communicate to your coach what goals you are seeking and he will be able to help you attain these goals. It is much easier for the coach to help someone who knows what he wants to learn or achieve. Depending on your skill level, you can accomplish these goals for yourself. You can set any goal in any situation and reach it. As soon as your goal is accomplished, start working on the next goal.

Now that you have made your wants or goals about yourself, you have control over your own life, and it is possible to work for what you want. Remember, anything is possible!

When selecting your goals or wants, Rule #2 indicates that you need to state your goal (what you want to do or accomplish) in positive terms. As individuals and athletes, we are very good at stating our wants in negative terms. For example, when thinking negatively, you might say, "I don't want to sit on the bench." Your thought of not wanting to sit on the bench is negative because that is what you fear, not what you want. Fear keeps you from thinking positively about what you want and only helps you to become more frustrated. You can work forever on all the things you don't want that are negative, or you can go for the goals that you want which are positive. A positive want would be, "I want to play."

Here are some specific examples of positive wants:

1. I want to be a starter.
2. I can improve my shooting percentage to a specific amount.
3. I want to concentrate on my passing.
4. I will get into my offensive or defensive position.

Now that you know the rules for making up your wants or goals, make your wants positive and about yourself. Remember, no goal is too high if you really want it. It does not matter why you want it, just that you want it. You don't need to justify why you want something.

Goals are the second step to *Thinking Straight*. Setting goals gives you self-direction which results in control over the way you want to perform. Goals keep you focused on what you want to do. Because you have goals, you will be more positive and not be discouraged by your own negative thoughts or by negative things that others might say. Since you will be working positively toward a goal, you will have a greater concentration to keep going for what you want. So many times you fumble around for solutions to problems that you encounter in situations which are important to you. When an athlete experiences a problem, many times he will avoid it or ignore it. Sometimes you will pretend that you don't have a problem. When you won't admit that you have a problem, it's a sure sign that you do have one. When you ignore or resist something, it will persist. The problem will continue to be there until it is resolved or until you decide to deal with it. To find temporary relief or to cope with the problem, many athletes or individuals turn to drugs, drinking, removing themselves through injuries or quitting the activity altogether because of the frustration. Sometimes you reach a point where all the frustration that you are experiencing is not worth it and you decide to remove yourself from the situation. This will give temporary relief from the problem, but you will need to work it out at some point in time. You can start by saying things to yourself like, "What do I want?" and, "Is this all worth it?"

Listening to your language and to your inner voice is the key to what you want. You need to pay attention to what you are saying to yourself and whether it is negative or positive. Are you saying things like, "I *wish* I could be a starter; I *hope* the coach notices; I *should* be starting; I *should* be a captain," or "I *hope* I shoot well tonight"? If you are hearing thoughts like these, chances are good that these things are what you really want. So, when you're ready, let's explore *accepting* what you want.

ACCEPTING WHAT YOU WANT

When you know what you want—accept it! Feel good about your choice for yourself. You deserve it! Remember, if you want something badly enough, you will do everything to get it. Knowing what you want and accepting what you want are two different concepts. Many times you may want something, but do little to achieve it. You are usually waiting for it to happen or for someone else to help you get it. And when and if you do receive it, you are amazed and surprised that you finally got what you had always wanted.

Accepting the idea of what you really want means actively moving and doing things to reach that goal. Intellectually, many players think they accept what they want. They make a noncommital statement of some sort like, "I want to be a starter." When you have accepted what you want, you will know it. It's not something that has to be stated, you will just know. And you will experience a good feeling within yourself. It's a feeling of confidence and assurance within you. You will say, "Yes, this is it!" You will feel as if no one can stop you, not even yourself. No one else can give this to you. It's your feeling and your feeling alone. You are in control of yourself.

Once you have decided specifically what you want, write it down. Keep this list with you and place it where you can see it every morning and night. Use a small card or piece of paper for your list and be specific.

Sample Cards for Listing Your Goals

> I am making it my intention to feel good
> about myself as a player and to work
> on one thing at a time.
> (Practices and games)

> I am making it my intention to play
> like a STARTER
> on the VARSITY TEAM
> (Practices and games)

> *Long Range Goals*
> Highest Scoring Average
> in Conference
> All Conference Player
> As Forward

Look at your goals every night before you go to bed. Reviewing your cards before you go to sleep will help your subconscious to continue working towards your goals. When you awake, realign your thoughts and intentions for working toward your goals by reviewing your goals and what you need to do to achieve them. Keep your list to yourself or you will waste energy by telling others what you are doing. Trying to impress others about what you are doing only means that you have not fully accepted what you want.

Now that you have set your goals and wants, you need to be open to new or different ideas. For example, if you want to have the highest scoring average in the conference, then find out what you need to do to achieve your goals. Remember, some people will do anything to get what they want, even lie and be dishonest. In T.S., we want to deal with truth and an honest way of getting what you want. So, how do you work towards your goal of having the highest scoring average in the conference?

First, you must find out specifically what you need to do to acquire the skills for whatever it is that you want. If it's a certain job, you need to go to your supervisor, and if it's in athletics, you need to go to your coach. Communicate to your supervisor or coach by asking for help and ideas that you can work on to assist you in reaching your personal goal. You need to be open and listen to what he has to say. Maybe you are thinking that you can't talk to your coach or boss, or you might be saying to yourself, "I could never do that!" Going to the coach or supervisor and communicating is what we mean by accepting what you want. You need to be willing to do everything it takes to reach that goal. Be open and listen to what the coach or boss has to say. If you are still saying you just can't talk to the coach or supervisor, then maybe you don't want to be the best shooter in the conference or the most successful in your field.

Perhaps after talking to the coach or boss, you realize that he doesn't really know exactly what to tell you to reach your goal. If you are committed to reaching your goal, you need to find someone or some way that can help you continue toward that goal. You need to do whatever it takes to keep working toward your goal. Maybe you could study from books or films or ask someone who knows the proper techniques so that you can practice them. Visualize yourself succeeding in those skills. Keep your eye on the goal.

Goals need to be set one step at a time. In order to accomplish what you want, you need to set specific goals. You want to set three types of goals: long, medium, and short-range. You need to set your specific goals at the beginning, middle, and toward the end of the season. You need to continually work toward being the best athlete (or coach) that you can be. This needs to be your overall goal. Coaches and athletes often set limits on themselves. Limits are restricting and keep us from being the best athlete or coach that we can be. Many times you might limit your goals by saving them for the future because you don't believe you can reach them now.

CHARACTER GOALS

To help you set goals for yourself, we have set the following goals for our eight T.S. characters.

Paul Putdown

Paul is always comparing himself with others and becomes self-destructive because he sees good qualities in others and faults in himself. He needs to focus on his strengths.

Paul's Goals Would Be:

Long-Range: To be the best 100 meter sprinter in the conference. (Results)

Medium-Range: (Practice and meets)
To cut time down to the nearest second.
To improve running form and body motions.

Short-Range: (Practice and meets)
To improve start form and quickness.
To improve leg strength using a weight program.
To run sprints.

Melissa Mistake

Melissa is afraid of making a mistake and focuses on her errors instead of thinking about what she does well. She needs to look ahead and see herself as a success.

Melissa's Goals Would Be:

Long-Range: To be one of the best single players and to win the conference singles title. (Results)

Medium-Range: (Practice and games)
To win the set.
To hit to opponent's backhand.
To vary strokes.

Short-Range: (Practice and games)
To take one game at a time.
To concentrate on serve.
To rush the net.

David Dolittle

David wants others to help him be successful and does very little work toward achieving his goals. He goes through the motions of doing the work. He needs to set step-by-step goals by taking responsibility for himself and by doing the work himself.

David's Goals Would Be:

- Long-Range: To play on the basketball team. (Results)
- Medium-Range: (Practice and games)
  To improve ballhandling, defense, and shooting.
- Short-Range: (Practice and games)
  To work on ballhandling three times a day.
  To work on dribbling drills three times a day.
  To work on shooting everyday for 30 minutes or more.
  To work on footwork drills 15 minutes a day.
  To play one on one three times a week concentrating on defense, shooting, and ballhandling.

Patty Perfect

Patty feels that she has to do everything perfectly before she can go on to her next goal. Nothing is good enough unless it is done correctly. She needs a pat on the back either from herself or from the coach. What she needs to realize is that no one is perfect and that everyone makes a mistake once in awhile.

Patty's Goals Would Be:

- Long-Range: To be a starting forward on the basketball team.
  To be all conference. (Results)
- Medium-Range: (Practice and games)
  To score 20 points a game.
  To average four steals a game.
  To get 18 rebounds a game.
- Short-Range: (Practice and games)
  To work on shooting 30 minutes a day.
  To work on defense and boxing out.
  To work on offensive moves to the basket.
  To work on fakes.

Rita Rescue

Rita is always helping everyone and ends up doing so many things for everyone else that she doesn't have time to do things for herself. She needs to set priorities and communicate her priorities to the other players so they can all work out a compromise.

Rita's Goals Would Be:

Long-Range:	To be a starter on the team as a forward. (Results)
Medium-Range:	(Practice and games)
	To be the fastest player on the team.
Short-Range:	(Practice and games)
	To work on ballhandling everyday.
	To work on sprints for speed.
	To work on passing.
	To work on fakes.

Willy Worry

Willy is always worrying about something. He tends to focus on the past or on future situations rather than on the present. Willy needs to direct his energy on one goal at a time and focus on what he is doing right now at the present time. Once he has achieved a goal he can set a new one.

Willy's Goals Would Be:

Long-Range:	To be a running back on the team. (Results)
Medium-Range:	(Practice and games)
	To gain three yards per carry.
	To develop quick moves.
Short-Range:	(Practice and games)
	To improve speed.
	To improve strength.
	To learn fakes and change of direction moves.
	To communicate with coach and players.

Brenda Blame

Brenda makes excuses when she does not accomplish her goals. She is always blaming others for her failures. Sometimes she doesn't know what to do, or if she does do something, she is afraid she will appear silly or different. Brenda needs to take responsibility for what she wants by improving her skills and communicate her wants. She needs to believe in herself.

Brenda's Goals Would Be:

Long-Range:	To be an all-around on the gymnastics team. (Results)

Goals: Finding Out What You Want

Medium-Range: (Practice and meets)
To work on intermediate routines daily.
To add difficulty when possible.

Short-Range: (Practice and meets)
To improve strength with a weight program.
To improve and maintain flexibility.
To practice handstand work on apparatus.
To work on tumbling drills daily.

Eddie Ego

Eddie knows what he wants, believes in himself and goes after it. Eddie usually is a challenge to his teammates and his coach. He has superior knowledge about the subject matter and goes for his goals. Eddie needs to communicate, continue to give input, and work on his own skills; then he will be able to work well with his coworkers.

Eddie's Goals Would Be:

Long-Range: To be a starting guard and leader on the basketball team.
To be all conference, all area, and all state.
(Results)

Medium-Range: (Practice and games)
To focus on his skills and game plan during the game.
To offer advice during the game.
To realize others have beliefs and opinions also and not let their's affect his play.

Short-Range: (Practice and games)
To work on his skills.
To be enthusiastic.

After you have set your goals, work at achieving them. Your goals will give you a positive attitude about what you want to achieve for yourself. They will give you self-direction and help you to concentrate on what you want. You need to have a personal commitment to your goals.

COMMITTING TO WHAT YOU WANT

A commitment is dedicating yourself totally to what you want. If you are going to make a commitment, then you will need to set priorities.

Priorities help you organize your schedule, give you the time to accomplish what you want to do and allow you to use your time more constructively. Make the most of the best and least of the worst.

You need to motivate yourself by saying, "No pain—no gain," or whatever works for you to keep you committed to your goals.

Keep in mind, though, that sometimes you may not know exactly what you want. You may think you want something and in the process of achieving your goal, you may find that you really want something else, or that you are not willing to work hard enough to reach a particular goal. So pick another goal. It's okay to change your mind. Maybe another goal is more important to you for now. The important thing is to stay with some type of goal and then you will always be moving towards positive growth. Through that growth you will experience that you can become the best person that you can be. If you want to stay with your goal, all you need to do is accept it and do whatever work needs to be done. Sound easy? It's not difficult to communicate, if the goal is what you really want. Sometimes it may seem difficult or even impossible to stay positive and committed to your goal. It's always easier to see our obstacles than it is to see our goals. Go ahead, go for it. Why not? You are not going to lose anything by going for it, and you won't feel any worse than you do right now! Go ahead, do it!

Now you need to work to achieve your goals.

DIRECT ALL ENERGY TOWARDS GETTING WHAT YOU WANT!

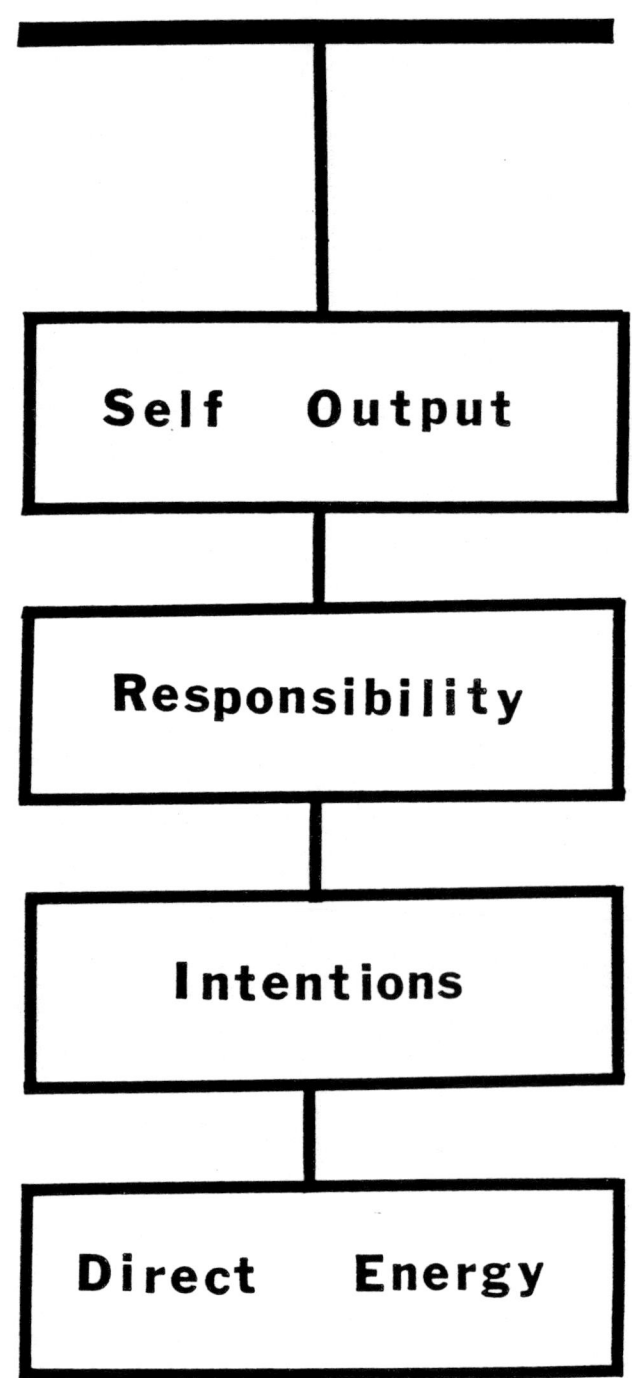

CHAPTER 5

WORK: DOING THE WORK

THE THIRD STEP TO T.S.

NOW THAT YOU have specific goals you want to achieve, you need to do the work to get what you want. If you are not willing to do the work for these goals or if you find yourself making excuses for why you can't attain these goals, maybe these goals are not the ones you want to achieve. You need to be willing to do whatever it takes to reach your goals. Sitting back wishing and hoping is not going to help you reach a higher scoring average or improve your passing.

After your coach or boss has given you the information that you need to work on, make it your intention to work on it every day during the practices or on the job. Direct all of your energies toward getting what you want. Work on one thing at a time and when you feel confident with that, move on to your next goal. It may take time, and if you are patient, persistent, and positive about your goal, then all your hard work will pay off. Part of doing the work also means doing the mental work.

David Dolittle is a person who doesn't do the work, but expects to reach his goals. He will dream about what he wants, but is not willing to do the work to attain those goals. He may even put forth a little effort and think he deserves to be successful. But without the work, he will be greatly disappointed and probably blame the coach or the other players for not getting what he wants or for not becoming successful. Blaming the coach can free him of any responsibility or work, but it won't get him what he wants.

Sometimes the coach or boss may not know exactly how to help you or tell you what you need to know to be the best person you can be. If you feel you are not getting the specific information that you need so you can start working on your goals, you need to find a source that does know exactly what needs to be done. If you really want to reach that goal, you will keep searching for someone or something that will give you positive directions toward your goals. Stay committed to that goal.

Once you have found the source for your information, be open, listen and pay attention to the information. Too often we think that our minds are capable of learning only one way to perform a task or skill. We can learn new and different skills. You can improve your performance by focusing on one skill at a time and practicing that skill every day. If you already believe in yourself and feel that what you are doing is right, then continue to believe it will work. Doing the work for someone else never works. You can only do the work for yourself.

ACHIEVING YOUR GOAL

After you have found out what to work on to reach your goal, you need to take 100 percent of the responsibility for achieving your goal. There are three steps you need to follow to take total responsibility.

1. Set Intentions.
2. Practice Self-Discipline.
3. Physically Work Towards Your Goal.

Step One: Set Intentions

When you set your intentions, you are really setting a pattern in your mind to perform the way you want, regardless of any distractions. You want to focus your intentions on the *result* you want to achieve.

Many times before an important event or game, you may feel nervous and excited about performing. Intentions will help you to concentrate on what you need to do and are specific reminders of what to concentrate on during your performance.

For example, during our basketball season we had a guard who occasionally had trouble shooting during the game. After analyzing her shot at practice, we discovered she was not completing her follow-through (motion after releasing the ball). When we discussed her shot with her, we found that under pressure as a defensive player was coming toward her, she would panic and just "chuck" (wildly throwing) the ball at the basket. She was concentrating on what the defensive player was doing, rather than on what she needed to be doing. She needed to set an intention for shooting. We decided her intention would be "following through." Each time she was going to shoot either in practice or games she was to say to herself the cue words, "Follow through." After setting her intentions she consistently averaged seventeen points a game. During the games she was able to concentrate on what she needed to do rather than on distractions such as her defensive opponent.

Some other specific intentions may be "Move my feet on defense," or "Snap my wrist when I pass the ball."

In order to set intentions, you need to have a picture in your mind of how to correctly perform the skill. The correct way to perform the skill can be found in fundamental skill books, video tapes, or live performances in your sport. Once you have decided on your intentions, focus your mind on the following sequence:

1. Remove yourself from busy and distracting areas and find a place of your own.

2. Sometime before the game or practice, get into a relaxed position, either sitting or lying down with your eyes closed. Concentrate on taking slow, deep breaths.

3. Relax your mind by thinking of a favorite place where you feel comfortable and happy. You need to concentrate on the muscles in your body until you can feel them becoming heavy and relaxed as if you are falling asleep. You need to tighten each muscle group and relax and imagine your body is full of sand that is sifting down to the ground each time you contract and relax. Start with your feet and move up to your head and face or start with your face and move down toward your feet. Tighten each group three to four times. Keep your mind on the process so that you can focus your mind. If you allow yourself to fall asleep, you will have mastered relaxation. Remember, however, that you need to stay awake to focus on your intentions!

4. Picture yourself in a game situation with positive action occurring around you. It's very important to have a mental picture of how to do the skill correctly. It is also important to picture yourself executing the skill with correct form.

For example, when you mentally picture yourself on the freethrow line, you need to see yourself shooting a freethrow, using the correct form and visualizing the ball going through the basket. Or you need to see yourself executing a difficult dismount from the high bar with a perfect landing, or successfully spiking the volleyball into your opponent's court.

5. Run the image of yourself performing the skill *correctly* and *successfully* through your mind ten times.

For example, you need to see yourself actually shooting a basketball and seeing your shot go through the basket. The sequence of this procedure needs to be free of interruptions. In other words, you want to keep the film running in your head to insure positive concentration.

The first time you use this process, do it before you go to bed, because it will take time to set up a routine for yourself. It also allows your subconscious to positively work out your situations. Go slow and take your time. Each time you repeat this procedure, you will find it becomes easier and almost an automatic process for you. Just thinking about your favorite place will set the process into motion.

There are three times that you will find visualizing intentions beneficial to your performance: before you go to sleep, before practice and games, and during the game. If you run through your intentions when you are sitting on the bench, when you get into the game your intentions will be set in your mind and you will find it easier to play like you want.

Step Two: Practice Self-Discipline

Self-discipline is a conscious effort to direct all your energies into the work involved in achieving your goal. Many times when going for your goal, you are wasting your energy without even knowing it.

In situations that are important to you, there are times when you are distracted and your energies are pulled from your goal and used on other things. Some of the situations distracting you from your goal might be hearing someone yell at you, listening to your peers, getting down on yourself, or worrying about other people and what they are saying. When you focus on these things instead of your goals, you tend to get frustrated and involved with the situation. Now you are using what we call negative energy. When you lose your self-discipline and begin to think about distractions, which are negative, you are no longer directing all your energy into achieving your goal. The key to self-discipline is to stay on target and work towards your goal, no matter what happens. When the negative energies pull you away from your goal, you need to focus your mind on yourself by asking, "What do I want and what are my intentions?" Do you want to work toward your goal, or do you want to be distracted by these other situations? By asking yourself these questions, you will become aware that you are wasting energy. This is negative because you are not working toward your goal. You need to make a continual, conscious effort to redirect your energy positively toward your goal. Say to yourself, "I can, I will and I want to reach my goals." Now you need to review your goals and visualize your specific intentions. By refocusing on your goal, you are now using what we call *positive energies*. If you choose the positive path, you will have more energy to apply getting what you want; you will achieve your goal sooner than if you choose the negative path. By choosing the positive path, you will become aware of all the possibilities and choices available to you for reaching your goal. At times it may be difficult to find a positive in your situation because the negatives are so strong. There is always something positive for you in any situation. It helps to look at the situation as a puzzle and think, "How can I turn this negative obstacle into something positive for me?" Focusing on the positive helps you to review your cue words and review your intentions.

For example, during a varsity basketball game, our point guard was unable to get to her position to run the offense, which was one of her goals. She was becoming frustrated by all the outside distractions of her teammates telling her what to do, the coach yelling instructions at her, and hearing the crowd's disapproval. She was beginning to use a lot of negative energy. She was losing her self-discipline and committed four turnovers in a row. Soon, she was so frustrated she couldn't even dribble the ball down the court. A time-out was called and we asked her, "What do you want?" She replied, "I don't know! I don't know! I can't dribble. Everyone is yelling at me." We said, "Well, think about what you want to do out there!" We said, "Can you do that?" She said, "I don't know!" Getting very specific on her goals, we asked her, "What do you need to do to set up the offense?" She replied, "Dribble the ball down the court." We asked her if she could do that and she said, "Yes!" Now she was beginning to use positive energy. Thinking positively as she was going back out into the game, she reviewed her specific intentions for dribbling, which were to keep her head up during dribbling and to protect the ball. As the game resumed, she was able to get to her offensive position. She regained her self-discipline and was able to control the offensive attack.

The following are some of the rewards you will experience when you gain self-discipline:

1. Gives you high energy.
2. Helps you feel you have control over yourself.
3. Helps you feel good about yourself.
4. Changes negative thinking to positive thinking.
5. Allows you to give 100 percent (which increases your chance of achieving your goals).

6. Utilizes your time effectively.
7. Carries over into your daily life situations.

Self-discipline is making up your mind to do something and letting nothing stop you from doing it, not even yourself.

Step Three: Physically Working Toward Your Goal

You can set all kinds of good intentions and visualize yourself being successful, but unless you are willing to do the physical work every day, you will not achieve your goal. No one can do the work for you, only you can do the work.

In every sport there are skills that need to be learned and perfected. Conditioning is one of the most important factors when learning skills. Without proper conditioning, the athlete becomes tired and fatigued while doing drills. As the athlete begins to fatigue, he becomes tired and performs the skills inaccurately. If the athlete practices the skills when tired, he becomes sloppy in execution and begins to practice bad habits. If a player continues to practice using bad habits, it will become more difficult to change, taking the player longer to correct his mistakes. As coaches, we all want the athletes to practice skill with correct form. It is for these reasons that an athlete needs to do a conditioning program.

Most good conditioning programs, depending on the sport, include:

1. Running sprints.
2. Jumping rope.
3. Lifting weights.
4. Running distance.
5. Doing aerobics.
6. Stretching.

Coaches will have specific ideas of what to add or delete from this program.

Conditioning can be boring. Knowing the benefits you will gain from doing the program helps make conditioning meaningful to you as an athlete. These benefits include:

1. Weights—makes you stronger and prevents injuries.
2. Sprints—increases your speed.
3. Jumping rope—increases your vertical jump.
4. Running distance—increases your endurance.
5. Aerobics—increases cardiovascular fitness.
6. Stretching—maintains your flexibility and helps prevent injuries.

What makes the difference? Conditioning:

When you're in the last quarter of the game, the score is tied, there are ten seconds on the clock and you steal the ball, you will be quick enough to beat your opponent down the floor and score the two points to win the game;

When you finish the last turn in your race, come into the straightaway and you are even with your opponents, you will be able to have that extra strength that you need for your kick to the finish line;

When the score is tied, an outside shot rebounds off the rim, and you and your opponent jump for the rebound both grabbing the ball in midair. On the way down, you will have the extra strength to pull the ball from your opponent's hands, regaining position of the ball, or

When, in the final volley of the set, your opponent hits several shots to your backhand, followed by a sharp cross court shot to your forehand, you will have the agility and footwork to return the shot for a point.

Conditioning makes the difference in your performance. How can you make conditioning the difference for you?

First, by knowing what the conditioning can do for you. If you understand the purpose of a program and how it will help you, you will be motivated to do the work.

Second, by experiencing (in a game situation) how conditioning can give you the edge over your opponent. Through practices and the games, you will feel yourself become physically stronger and quicker.

Third, by helping you to perform the way you want to all the time. By focusing on yourself and on how you are improving as an individual or as a team member, conditioning will become fun for you.

If you can visualize conditioning as a positive step toward getting what you want, you will have made conditioning the difference for you.

Along with conditioning, you need to work on your skills everyday.

Daily drills in practice isolate the skills to be learned; repetition helps you to focus on that specific skill. Drills give you choices and alternatives that you can use during practices by setting an intention for each drill. In other words, what specifically do you want to work on when going through this drill? If you don't know the areas in which you want to improve, then you are going through the motions of doing the work.

By knowing what you want to work on and by focusing on these specific skills, practices will be intense, taking less time to do the drills, and skills will be performed correctly. Practices with purpose will accomplish more in a shorter period of time.

You need to look at practices and games as opportunities to continue to work on the way you want to perform. Too many times in a game a missed shot is looked at as a loss of points instead of as an opportunity to continue to focus on your specific skill of shooting just as you did in practice.

The more often you look at practices and games as the same situation, the sooner the intention you use in practices will carry over into your game. You will be able to perform the way you want more consistently.

It's hard to be intense all the time. Sometimes when the work seems hard or difficult, it's easy to slack off, stop working, or quit. When the work seems like the same old thing and it's not fun anymore, you have stopped working on your goals. If you really want to meet your goals, then why settle for less than what you can really accomplish?

If your practice is not designed to help you work on the specific skills you need to improve, then you need to communicate with your coach. First, you need to be clear on what it is that you want to do in practice that will help you. Second, you need to set up a time other than practice time when you can talk to the coach. Third, be willing to state your goals to the coach.

If, after communication with the coach, you are still not getting to work on what you need, do it on your own time for as long as you want.

There is no way of getting around it; you need to do the work to get what you want.

THERE ARE NO LIMITS...
WHEN IT COMES TO GOING FOR WHAT YOU WANT!

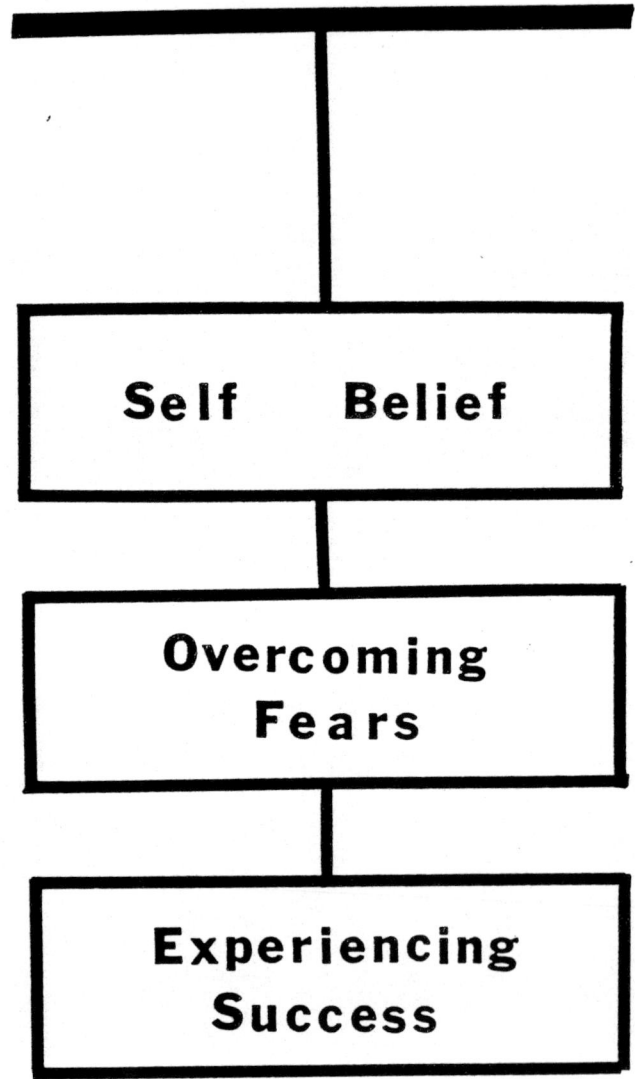

CHAPTER 6

RISK: CONQUERING YOUR FEAR OF FAILURE

THE FOURTH STEP TO T.S.

NOW THAT YOU have learned how to communicate your specific goals (what you want) and have worked toward those goals (accepting what you want), you need to be willing to risk and experience the total growth of being the best person that you can be.

Risking is being yourself and doing whatever you want at the moment. It is being yourself no matter who you are with or what you are doing. For the moment, we mean what you are choosing to do right *now*. What you have chosen is exactly what you want, otherwise you would be doing something else. It is helpful to think of things happening to ourselves as a choice, rather than just something that happens for no reason. If things do not turn out the way you think they should, you might start to blame others. You do this so you don't have to take responsibility for the things or happenings in your life. Blaming others also wastes a great amount of energy that could be used working toward your goals. It makes no sense in blaming the coach, Mom, Dad, or anyone else; you have made the choice. For example, you may be choosing to be a good friend to a teammate by passing the ball to him rather than going for your own goal of shooting the ball and scoring your point average. If your teammate misses the shot, you may find yourself getting angry or upset with him. Because you chose to be what you thought was a good friend rather than going for what you wanted, you are blaming something outside yourself for ruining your opportunity to score or maintain your point average. Instead of immediately passing the ball to a teammate, because you are a team player, you need to think, "Shoot the ball first." You need to give yourself the opportunity to shoot first if the chance is there. By passing the ball to your teammate before considering yourself, you have eliminated one of your choices. You will always want to pass the ball to a teammate; your risk is to think about yourself first. You must take responsibility for your choices. You will then realize that you can also make different choices and you will have the ability to even change your choices if you don't like what is happening.

A risk is doing something that you haven't been able to do in the past or at the moment. Risking is vital in experiencing the fifth and final step of *Thinking Straight*. By risking, you can learn to overcome your fears and gain self-confidence so that you can attain your goals. When believing in yourself, you will experience the success of achieving each of your goals.

No risk is the same for everyone. What seems to be a small risk for one person may be a tremendous risk for another person. Choosing other choices may be risky for you. Some people feel that a risk is taking a chance. A risk needs to be positive and something you feel will be good for you. It needs to be something that is not going to harm you or others. All of us know what would be a risk for ourselves. Sometimes you may not be consciously aware of the risk or of what you know. You may try to deny knowing your risk, but at some level of awareness you know what your risk would be. You have a feeling inside of yourself that signals to you when you are aware of what you know. How can you become more aware of your own risk?

You need to start asking yourself questions and start becoming aware of what you are thinking:

1. "What do I want?" Remember, make your want positive and about yourself. If you don't know specifically what it is that you want, then you will not be able to take a risk.

2. "Do I know what I need to do to get what I want?" If you don't know, then find out!

3. "Do I want it badly enough to do the work or whatever is required to get what I want?" How badly do you want it?

4. "Am I going to choose to do it right now?" What are you waiting for?

Are you making excuses?

Would This Be a Risk for You?

1. Telling your coach how you feel about practices, what you want to work on in practice, your thoughts about the previous game, that you want to play more often or just telling him anything.

2. Going with what you feel is right at the moment, during the game situation, rather than with the coach's original instructions for the game plan.

3. Telling the other players how you feel about certain situations that have occurred during the games or practices.

How do you know what is a risk for you? You know it is a risk when you hear yourself saying, "No way; I could never do that. Can't I do something else, something easier?" If you are committed to your goals, you need to take the risk. Without the risk, you will have difficulty reaching all of your goals. Risking is difficult and sometimes scary and uncomfortable. It is always easier to stay with the same way of doing things or with the old way of thinking than to venture into something new and different. When staying with the old or comfortable way, you will remain at the same performance level that you are right now. For example, if you are a basketball player and now shoot 20 percent from the floor, unless you risk by changing your shooting technique or by shooting more often, you will remain a 20 percent shooter. If you are content with being a 20 percent shooter, then you don't need to change anything. Your risk is to stay the way you are, regardless of what anyone says about your shooting, even the coach. Maybe the goal is just to be a part of the team and not a good shooter. If your goal is to be a good shooter, 50 percent or more, then your risk is to change your shooting technique or shoot more often. If you choose to go with a new shooting technique, you need to stay committed to it and use it everyday. You need to be patient, use your visual imagery and see yourself successfully performing your shot with the new shooting technique. There may be times when you experience a drop in your performance level. Maybe now instead of shooting 20 percent, you are only shooting 10 percent in practice or games. The drop in your performance is not because the new technique doesn't work; it's because you are beginning to think about other things. You begin to doubt yourself and worry about what others are saying about you. The risk is to stay positive and committed to your goal, no matter what. Often a player will quit using the new technique or say, "I can't use this shot," instead of being patient and working through the period of feeling uncomfortable. To work through the uncomfortable feeling, you need to focus on the new shooting technique and keep using it until you experience success in your practices and game situations. You will have a feeling of self-confidence and you will be able to overcome your fear of missing the basket. You will experience an increase in your shooting percentage which can only be limited by a change in your thinking or in your commitment.

In coaching situations, we have found that an athlete who has been using the new techinque successfully in practices may revert back to his old technique in a game or meet situation. This regression happens for two reasons:

1. When something becomes important to you, you tend to go with the old and familiar, something that worked for you in the past.

2. When you focus on your fears, you start thinking about what you can't do, instead of knowing what you can do.

Figure 12. The Wall of Frustrations

The Wall

By focusing on your fears, you will create failures and keep yourself from experiencing success. What is it like when you are experiencing your fear of failure? You may feel uncomfortable, teary-eyed, frustrated, and have a desire to escape from the situation. You may also hear yourself saying negative things about yourself and others like, "I don't want to talk to the coach; I don't like the officials; I don't want to sit on the bench;" or "I can't shoot." All of these feelings bring you to a frustration level which we refer to as *The Wall*. The wall is a point where you stop yourself from going for what you want. You stop yourself from risking because your fear is greater than your desire to get what you want. The wall contains the athlete's fears, such as: worrying about hurting a teammate's feelings; hoping the coach doesn't yell at you; worrying if you will perform well, or thinking, "Am I as good as the newspapers say I am?" or "What will my parents think of me?" The wall exists because of all the negative things that you are telling yourself, things which are a waste of time and energy.

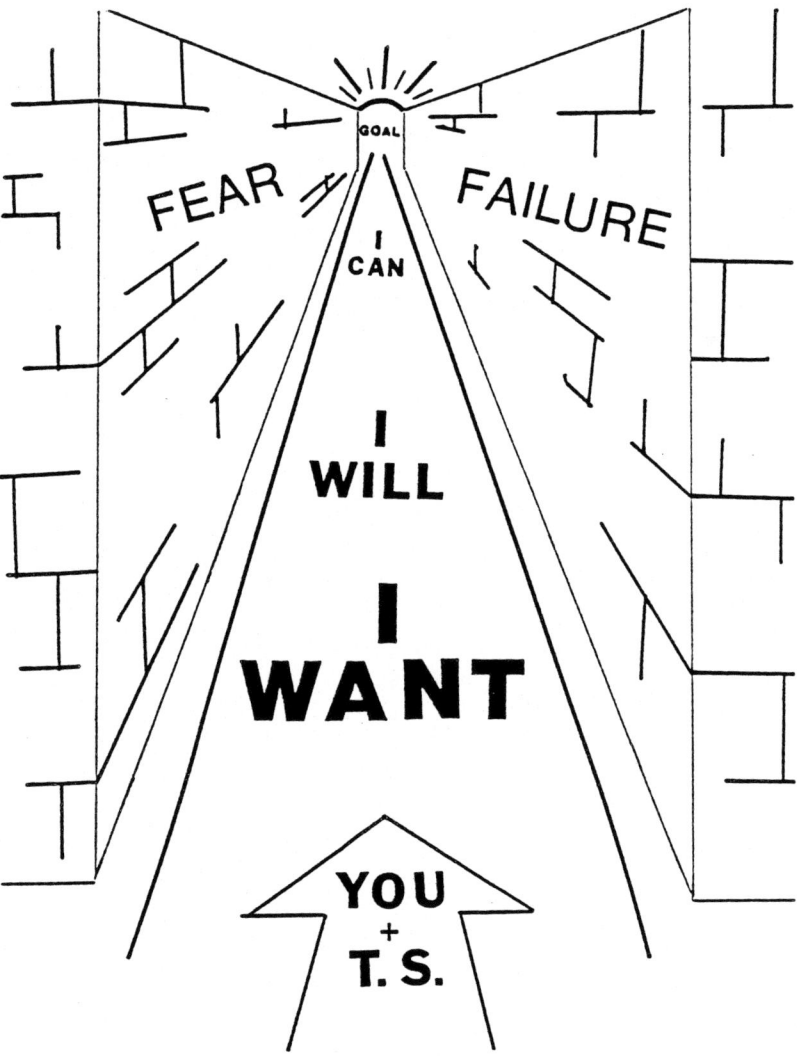

Figure 13. Fear of Failure

In order to overcome your fear of failure and go through the wall, you need to:

1. Be clear on exactly what your goal is.
2. Think positive! Think I CAN, I WILL, I WANT toward your goal.
3. Take positive action toward that goal!

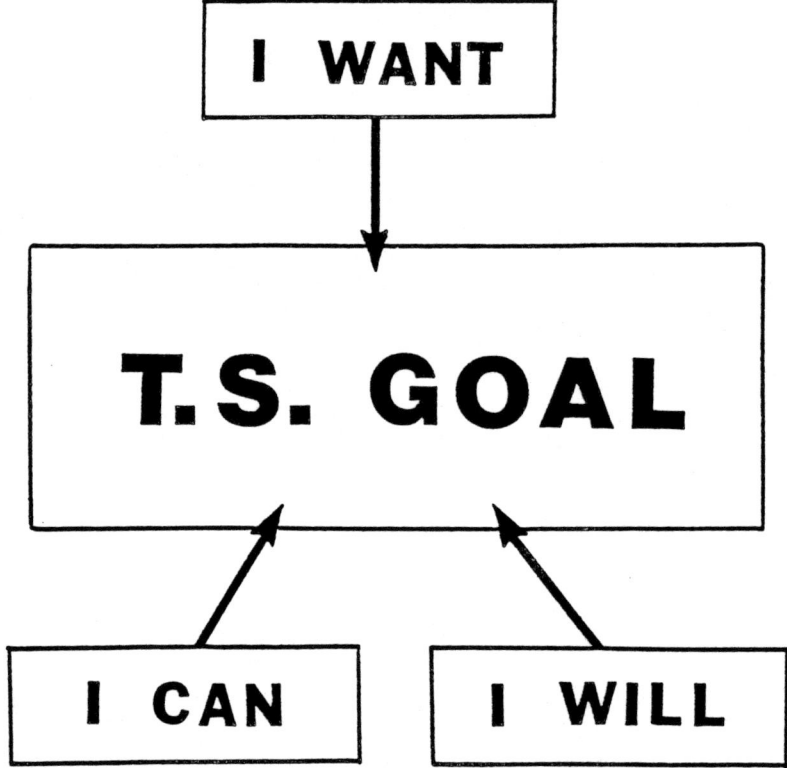

Figure 14. Overcoming Fear of Failure

When you take a risk, you experience that your fear of what you think could happen is far greater than what actually happens or occurs. By visualizing yourself successfully taking the risk, you will create your goals rather than your failures. Using your visual imagery daily will help you to direct yourself in a positive way toward your goals.

The risk is the same for all of us. You need to:

1. Know what you want!
2. Concentrate on the specific techniques for your skill.
3. Focus on one thing at a time.
4. Take action — do it!

CHARACTER RISKS

Let's look at what a risk would be for each one of our eight T.S. characters (for character definitions refer to Chapter 2).

Paul Putdown

Paul's risk is to stay centered on himself by developing a mental routine (visual imagery, etc.) that he can use before each practice and meet. By focusing on his strengths, he will then be able to run the race he wants to run. He needs to ignore the other runners and focus on himself before and during the race so that he can concentrate on each of his coaching tips. He can socialize after the race.

Melissa Mistake

Melissa's risk is to concentrate positively on her game plan. If she makes a mistake, she needs to forget it and focus on her strategy for the next play.

David Dolittle

David's risk is to take responsibility for himself. To develop his skills, he needs to do his daily work and work on one thing at a time.

Patty Perfect

Patty's risk is to perform her skill and not worry about the execution of the skill. She needs to realize that she is good enough just the way she is.

Rita Rescue

Rita's risk is to give herself permission to do what she wants to do. She needs to set priorities and make time for herself.

Willy Worry

Willy's risk is to focus specifically on his goal or on what he is doing right now.

Brenda Blame

Brenda's risk is to take responsibility for her goals by working on her skills and communicating to others what she wants.

Eddie Ego

Eddie's risk is to say to himself, "It's okay to be a superstar." He needs to continue working toward his goals and communicating with his teammates and coach.

By taking the risk of going for what you want, you will feel good about yourself and be able to focus positively on all your strengths. You will experience happiness and personal growth and, finally, you will experience *Thinking Straight*.

"AWESOMIDITY"
FEELING AWESOME TO THE POINT OF SATURATION!

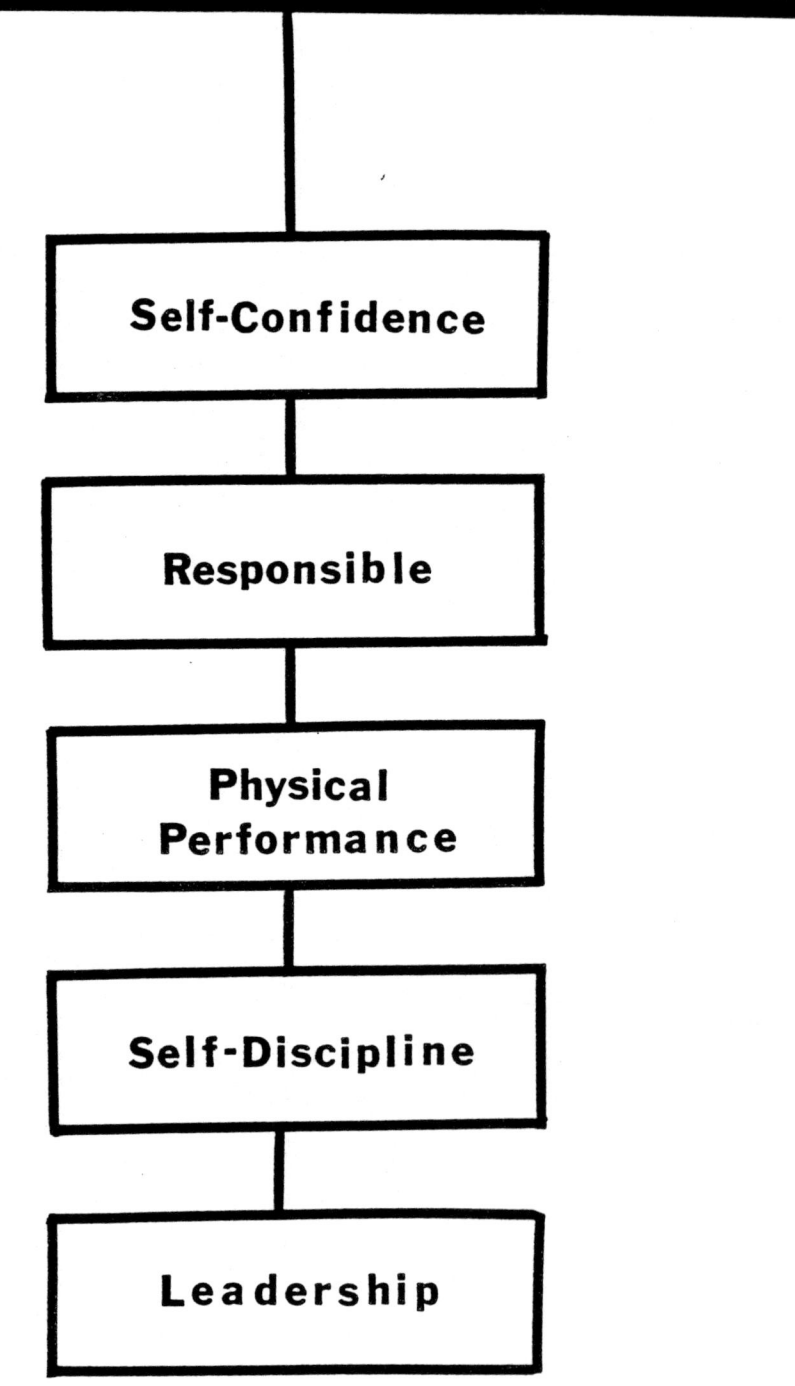

CHAPTER 7

GROWTH: THE FUN OF IT!

WHEN WE GET what we want, we are happy. As Lao-tzu said over 2500 years ago, "A journey of a thousand miles must begin with a single step." When you are happy, you begin to enjoy what we call *the fun of it*. Let's look at what the fun of it has been for us and can be for you.

You, too, can experience what we call *awesomidity*. Awesomidity is feeling awesome to the point of saturation. The awesome feeling you experience comes from growth, the end result of *Thinking Straight*. You can use all or any part of T.S. and experience some success or use all the steps of T.S. and experience personal growth, success, and happiness. In order to experience the total feeling of T.S., you need to risk and break through the wall. When you have experienced going through the wall, you will know how to get through it again when it reappears. When you are going for your personal goals there will always be a wall (risks) that you will need to go through to get what you want.

CHARACTER GROWTHS

Since you will always be one or more of the T.S. characters at any given moment, you will know how to make better choices for yourself throughout your life. Each of the eight T.S. characters are within all of us. Your behavior depends on which one you are acting out at the moment. In other words, you can be a Patty Perfect at work and a Paul Putdown on the soccer field. Or you may be a Rita Rescue at home and an Eddie Ego on the basketball court. You will always be the same type of character in similar situations throughout your life. So now that you know the risk and what it takes to go through the wall, you will be able to live a happier life.

Here are some of the T.S. Experiences that were fun for us:

Paul Putdown

There was a talented sprinter on the track team who was not performing to the best of his ability. At the starting blocks, he would find himself focusing on the other runner's body build and talents, rather than on himself. Even during the race, he was thinking about the other runners catching up to him. After using T.S., he was able to concentrate on his running techniques and focus on what he wanted to do during the race. He felt good about himself as a runner because he was running to the best of his ability and this helped him to win more races.

Melissa Mistake

One of the varsity tennis players was playing first doubles for the first time in a big meet. Previously, she had been a consistent winner in the second doubles position. She didn't believe she was good enough to play first doubles and began to think negatively. She was thinking about all the mistakes she was going to make in the meet. After using T.S., she was able to focus her intentions on how she wanted to perform during the meet. She was then able to play the way she wanted and beat her opponent.

David Dolittle

One of our varsity forwards had high expectations of herself for the season. She would see herself as a superstar. In her desire to prove herself during games, she would attempt to do everything, causing her to appear as if she was wildly out of control. It was so important for her to show the coach that she could do the job, that she often forgot about her part in the game plan or with her teammates. The player felt she was playing great. The coach was frustrated because she knew the player was going through the motions during drills at practice. During games, the coach and team became frustrated because the game plan was not being run.

The coach sat down with the player and told her specifically what she needed to work on during practices. The coach and player designed specific step by step goals for daily work. By setting specific goals, it helped the player to take responsibility for doing the work and to improve her skills. The coach felt good about herself for helping the player and now could focus on her own goals for the team and game plan.

The player, after taking responsibility for herself, felt better about herself as a player because she actually improved her skills and made a valuable contribution to the team.

Patty Perfect

We had a forward on the varsity basketball team who felt she must have a perfect shot before she could shoot in a game. She felt that if she took the place of someone else on the court and missed her shot, others would think she was not good enough to be playing on the varsity team. She thought the other players on the team could do a better job of shooting than she could. She felt that she would hurt the team if she shot and missed. After using T.S., she realized she needed to forget about what other people might think and just concentrate on her shot. When she missed a shot, she realized that no one is perfect and that everyone makes a mistake once in a while. Once she realized this, she was able to shoot and play consistently.

Rita Rescue

We had a guard on the varsity basketball team who wanted to make basketball her first priority, and her family wanted her to make the family her first priority. She felt she had to babysit, clean the house, and do family-oriented things. She became frustrated as a player and as a person. After using T.S., by setting priorities, she gained control of her life and was able to take responsibility to get what she wanted. She improved tremendously as a basketball player and also was able to spend more quality time with her family.

Willy Worry

We worked with an outstanding senior football player who began to drop every pass that was thrown to him. He felt like he didn't have enough time to catch the ball. After talking, we found out that he was worried about his homework, getting good grades, getting a scholarship for college, and doing well in football. Everthing he did was becoming a "have to" for him. After using T.S., he was able to focus on one thing at a time. In the following game, he caught every pass and felt as if the ball were in slow motion. He felt he had all the time in the world to catch the ball. He also found time to do his homework and increase his chances for a scholarship.

Brenda Blame

One of our gymnasts was working to become an all-around gymnast on the team. As her performances became weaker, she began to make excuses to cover up her mistakes. She began to blame the coach for not spending as much time with her as he did with the other gymnasts.

Instead of concentrating on her skills, she spent most of her practice time complaining. After using T.S., our gymnast started to take responsibility by working daily on her individual skills. She also communicated with the coach when she needed help or advice. She started to believe in herself again and her performance improved.

Eddie Ego

We had a guard on the varsity basketball team who, year after year, would often challenge and sometimes frustrate the coach. During practices, she would always want to know what we were going to do and often had her own ideas of what the team needed to cover. Because she had advanced skills and learned things quickly, she often became impatient with other team members who needed more time to practice.

During games, because she actually did know what needed to be done, she would sometimes tell the coach what plays to run. For example, she would say, "Coach, its time to run a stall!" Before using T.S., the coach found herself frustrated by the player's suggestions and would either say, "No, we will run play five," or would remove the player from the game, even if the player was right.

After applying T.S., the coach was open to suggestions from the players. Even though the coach may not have used the suggestions, she always seriously considered their possibility. Because of the openness of the coach, the players felt free to communicate their perceptions of the game or practice. It helped the coach and team stay clear on their game plan and developed greater team cohesion.

PERSONAL GROWTHS

It was rewarding to see our players communicate and care about each other on and off the court. The caring developed and they realized they could not blame anyone but themselves for anything they were not getting. Each player knew what he needed in order to get what he wanted. They actually felt good about themselves as players and as people. The players were so intense during their practices that we, as coaches, found that we could develop more options for our offense, run more drills, and could teach them a variety of presses and defenses. As coaches, we were challenged to be the best coaches that we could be. Coaching became fun. The fun of using *Thinking Straight* was seeing the players start believing in themselves, improving their physical performance, gaining control of their thoughts and realizing that they could get what they wanted from their sport. They also realized that they did make a difference to the team. Some of the less confident players who had been intimidated by the coach turned into players that knew what they wanted and believed that it was up to themselves to go after what they wanted.

One of the biggest advantages that we found in the *Thinking Straight* approach to athletics is that there are virtually no limits when it comes to going for what you want. Once you have experienced *Thinking Straight*, your realm of possibility in getting what you want will grow enormously.

Here is a list of some of the positive things we experienced using the T.S. process:

1. Open communication grew between players and coaches.
2. Individual growth of players, physically and mentally, developed.
3. A higher energy level at practices and games was evident.
4. Ability to cope with official's calls, parents, side line coaching, and home pressures became more natural.
5. Peer pressure was dealt with in a positive manner.
6. Coaches were able to participate with the players as a team member rather than as an outside dictator.
7. Individuals felt good about themselves.
8. Individuals made cognitive, positive choices.
9. Players took responsibility for their own growth.
10. Players decided what they wanted from a sport.
11. Players developed values for daily life situations.
12. Individual statistics increased.
13. Team statistics increased.
14. Win-loss records improved.
15. Players changed negative thinking into positive thinking during the game.

In the past, as teachers and coaches, we have helped individuals improve in their skills and enjoy their sport. The feeling that we make a difference in their lives is one of the main reasons we stay in our profession. No matter what sport we coach, we always find that we need to work with the Willy Worrys, Melissa Mistakes and Patty Perfects. When working with these players in the past, we used to feel frustrated because we did not know how to help them play to their potential. Our belief was, "A good coach could help players become the best players that they could be." Now, after using the T.S. approach to athletics, we have found that no matter what type of player we are working with, we can make a difference in their physical performance, as well as in their personal lives.

One of the biggest advantages of using the *Thinking Straight* approach is that there are no limits when it comes to going for what you want. Once you experience T.S., your realm of possibilities of getting what you want are endless.

We observed that players were able to communicate with the other players by using the T.S. language. An example of how teammates might use T.S. language to support one another follows:

Mid-season, two players are talking in the locker room. Player #1 is frustrated and is not getting what he wants out of the season. Player #2 is getting what he wants by using T.S.

Player #1: "I'm frustrated this season. I never get to play. I haven't played in the last four games. The coach is playing someone else in my position and I know I can play better than him."

T.S. Player: "Have you talked to the coach? If you want to play, you need to tell the coach."

Player #1: "I did, and he said I needed more work on defense."

T.S. Player: "Have you been working?"

Player #1: "Yeah, I've been doing all the drills and working on skills."

T.S. Player: "Do you believe you're good enough to play?"

Player #1: "Yes, but the coach doesn't!"

T.S. Player: "No, you are the one that doesn't believe that you are good enough. You're just blaming the coach. You're saying, 'I'll believe in myself when the coach puts me in the game.' You're waiting for the coach to say when your defense is good enough for you to play. You need to believe in yourself. Get off of the coach's approval. What does it mean if you play? Does it mean you are a more valuable person?"

Player #1: "Well, I want to make a contribution to the team."

T.S. Player: "You make a contribution now!"

Player #1: "How?"

T.S. Player: "By being part of the team and participating at practice."

Player #1: "Yeah, you're right! I am waiting for the coach's approval. I'm going to go back to the coach and ask what specific goals I can work on."

Player #1's belief is that he needs the coach's approval in order to believe he is a good player.

ATHLETIC GROWTHS

The following examples are of players who knew what they wanted and were committed to reaching their goals:

T.S. Experience #1

We had a situation with one of our players, Mary, during practice. Mary wanted Jane to work with her on one of her new plays for the next game. Jane wanted to work on her freethrows. Even though Jane's good friend Mary wanted Jane to help her, Jane needed to be focused and to continue to direct all her energies on her freethrows. Even if she had decided to help Mary, she would not have been very effective because Jane's mind would have been on her freethrows instead of on helping her friend. Remember, you need to direct all your energies to what you want and not to what others want you to do. Only after Jane got what she wanted could she effectively help Mary. In the next game, Jane was sent to the freethrow line twelve times. Because she centered on herself at practice, she was able to do what she wanted. She shot 80 percent from the line that night. As for Mary, if she had really wanted help with her new play, she would have kept directing her energies to finding someone who would eventually help her.

T.S. Experience #2

Sometimes during a game, the opponents will do anything to get what they want. For example, we had a key player who was becoming frustrated during the game because the opponents were pushing, holding, and verbally trying to distract her. Our player began to foul and lose her concentration and composure. We took the player aside and helped her to realize that what was taking place on the court was about them. They did not believe in their ability to get what they wanted in the game against her. They felt the only way they had a chance to win was by holding, pushing, and verbally distracting her. When she realized that she was focused on the other players instead of on herself, she could refocus on her intentions and go for what she wanted in the game. Although she had three fouls and was distracted the first half of the game, our player was able to play the entire second half and still finish with her scoring average of 15 points. In the past, our player would become frustrated and did foul out of the game.

T.S. Experience #3

One year our game plan was to use a run and gun offense. In order for the players to execute this offense well, they needed to run "suicide" line drills or sprint exercises to develop conditioning. Most players think of line drills as a *have to* because they have been told by the coach that they need to do them. Lines become a have to because the players think of all the negative things about lines, like the pain, the fatigue and the difficulty in executing them, especially at the end of practice. When you hear yourself saying, "I have to run suicide lines," you need to be aware that this is a reminder that you need to do the work to get what you want. You need to ask yourself, "What do I want?" If you really want to be a better player and execute the fast break of run and gun offense well, then you need to do the work of running the lines and think of the positive things that this work is going to get you. As soon as our team experienced this thinking, our players were able to play the fourth quarter almost as fresh as they played their first quarter. It was difficult for the opponents to keep up with our fast break offense. The players experienced that they were in better condition for our running game and could do what was planned.

The ultimate goal of T.S. is to use the process to become a whole brain thinker. Whole brain thinking allows you to blend physical and mental activity to reach your maximum potential. You can have complete control of your performance to a point where you are unaware of anything around you. T.S. helps you to be a whole brain thinker by controlling how you communicate, knowing you can achieve your goals, experiencing that working toward your goal is fun, taking the risk to go for what you want and, finally, experiencing the success that you created for yourself.

When you experience T.S., you can apply it to all parts of your life, not just athletics, and that's the real fun of it!

Remember, all you need to do is have the wisdom to know what you want, the courage to accept what you want, and the strength to go after it. As we say to ourselves and our players, "What are you waiting for? Go for it! You deserve it!"

T.S. We love you.

WHEN WE GET WHAT WE WANT, WE ARE HAPPY!

REFERENCES

Alberti, Robert E. and Emmons, Michael L. *Your Perfect Right.* San Luis Obispo, CA: Impact, 1982.

Ballard, Jim. "Addicted to Success? Maybe Win-Win is the Game You've Always Wanted to Play," 1980.

Barnlund, Dean C. *Perspectives on Communication.* C.E. Larson and F.E.X. Dance (eds.), Madison, WI: Helix Press, 1968.

Berglund, Dean C. "Communication: The Content of Change." *Basic Readings in Communication Theory.* C. Mortensen, p. 16, 1979.

Bird, Anne Marie. "Development of Model for Predicting Team Performance." *Research Quarterly for Exercise and Sport.* 1977, pp. 24-32.

Bird, Anne Marie. "Team Structure and Success as Related to Cohesiveness and Leadership." *Journal of Social Psychology.* 1977, pp. 217-223.

Blanchard, Kenneth and Johnson, Spencer. *The One Minute Manager.* New York, Berkley, 1984.

Bristol, Claude M. *The Magic of Believing.* Englewood Cliffs, NJ: Prentice-Hall, 1969.

Burns, David D. M.D. *Feeling Good: The New Mood Therapy.* New York: New York American Library, 1971.

Chase, Larry M.D. "The Power of Belief." *Basic Responsibility.* 1980.

Clevenger, Theodore Jr. and Matthews, Jack. *The Speech Communication Process.* Glenview, IL: Scott, Foresman, 1971.

Danielson, R.R., Zelhard Jr., P.F. and Drake, C.J. "Multidimensional Scaling and Factor Analyses of Coaching Behavior as Perceived by High School Hockey Players." *Research Quarterly for Exercise and Sport,* 1975, pp. 323-334.

Dewey, John. *Experience and Nature.* LaSalle, IL: Open Court, 1925, p. 246.

Dwyer, Dr. Wayne. *Your Ennoneous Zones.* New York: Funk and Wagnalls, Sept. 1977, p. 82.

Ellis, Albert. *A New Guide to Rational Living.* Cedar Knolls, NJ: Wehmn, 1980.

Fielder, F.E. *A Theory of Leadership Effectiveness.* New York: McGraw-Hill, 1967.

Hagstrom, W.O. and Selvin, H.C. "The Dimensions of Cohesiveness in Small Groups." *Sociometing,* 1965. pp. 30-43.

Hoover, Thomas. *The Zen Experience.* New York: New American Library, 1980.

Jampolsky, Gerald G. *Love Is Letting Go Of Fear,* New York, Bantam, 1981.

Lawther, John. *Sport Psychology.* Prentice-Hall, Englewood Cliffs, NJ: 1972.

Martins, R. and Peterson, J. "Group Cohesiveness as a Determinant of Success and Members in Team Performance," *International Review of Sport Sociology*, 1971, pp. 49-61.

Mortensen, C. David. *Basic Reading in Communication Theory.* New York: Harper and Row, 1979.

Patent, Arnold M. *You Can Have It All,* Money Mastery, Piermont, New York, 1984.

Penman, K.A., Hastad, D.N. and Cords, W.L. "Success of the Authoritarian Coach," *Journal of Social Psychology,* 1974, pp. 155-156.

Sherrod, Barbara. "Jobs for Left and Right Brainers," *Illinois Career Magazine,* Curriculum Innovations, Vol. 14, No. 3, November 1985, p. 19.

Smith, R.E., Smoll, F.L. and Curtis, E.C. "Systems for the Behavioral Assessment of Athletic Coaches," *Research Quarterly for Exercise and Sport.* 1977, pp. 401-407.

Whitmont, Edward C. *Return of the Goddess.* New York: Crossroad, 1986.

Wilson, Colin. *Frankenstein's Castle: The Right Brain: Door to Wisdom.* Bath, Arron Great Britain: Ashgrove, 1980.

Zdenek, Marilee. *The Right Brain Experience.* New York: McGraw-Hill, 1983.

INDEX

A

Alberti, Robert E., 85
Awesomidity, definition, 73, 75

B

Ballard, Jim, 85
Barnlund, Dean C., 9, 85
Basketball practice, sports dialogue, 37-38
Bird, Anne Marie, 85
Blanchard, Kenneth, 85
Brain functions
  left brain functions (*see* Left brain dominance)
  right brain functions (*see* Right brain dominance)
  whole brain thinking (*see* Whole brain thinking)
Brandstat, Gloria, xi
Bristol, Claude M., 85
Brongiel, Geri, xi
Brown, Barbara, 9
Burns, David D., 85

C

Characters of thinking straight
  Brenda Blame
    characteristics, 18, 25-26, 50
    goals for, 50-51
    growth of, 78
    illustration, 25
    risks for, 72
  David Dolittle
    characteristics, 17, 20-21, 48
    goals for, 49
    growth of, 76-77
    illustration, 21
    risks for, 71
    work and, 55
  Eddie Ego
    characteristics, 18, 26-27, 51
    goals for, 51
    growth of, 75, 78
    illustration, 27
    risks for, 72
  Melissa Mistake
    characteristics, 17, 19-20, 48
    goals for, 48
    growth of, 76, 80
    illustration, 20
    risks for, 71
  Patty Perfect
    characteristics, 17, 21-22, 49
    goals for, 49
    growth of, 75, 77, 80
    illustration, 22
    risks for, 21
  Paul Putdown
    characteristics, 17, 18-19, 48
    goals for, 48
    growth of, 75, 76
    illustration, 18, 19
    risks for, 71
  Rita Rescue
    characteristics, 18, 22-23, 49
    goals for, 50
    growth of, 75, 77
    illustration, 23
    risks for, 71
  Willy Worry
    characteristics, 18, 24-25, 50
    goals for, 50
    growth of, 77, 80
    illustration, 24
    risks for, 71

Chase, Larry, 85
Choices for self, 7-13
　making changes, 9
　making choices, xiii
　of coaches, 7-8
　of players, 7-8
　options, 8
　selection immediate goal, 9
Clevenger, Theodore, Jr., 85
Communication
　self-talk, 31-38 (*see also* Self-talk)
　sports dialogues, 37-38
　　basketball practice, 37-38
　　football, 37
　　volleyball practice, 38
　structure, diagram, 30
　use of, 7
Conditioning
　benefits of, 60
　differences made by, 61-62
　program for, 60, 61
Cords, W.L., 86
Curtis, E.C., 86

D

Dance, F.E.X., 85
Danielson, R.R., 85
Danish, Steven J., 32
Dewey, John, 9, 85
Drake, C.J., 85
Dwyer, Wayne, 85

E

Ellis, Albert, 85
Emmer, Pam, xi
Emmons, Michael L., 85

F

Fielder, F.E., 85
Football, sports dialogue, 37

G

Goals
　acceptance of what is wanted, 45-47
　as positive, 44
　　examples, 44
　attainability of goals, 47-51
　character goals, 47-51
　commitment to, 51-52
　examples, 43
　for yourself, 41-42
　　illustration, 43
　importance communicating with others, 41
　key to thinking straight, chart, 6
　openness to new and different ideas, 46-47
　physical work toward, 60-62 (*see also* Work)
　problems relating to, 41-42, 44-45
　purpose, 7
　rules for, 42
　selection immediate goal, 9
　structure, diagram, 40
　types of, 47
　use of, xiv
　"want" defined, 42
　writing goals on cards, 45
　　illustration, 46
　　use of, 46
Growth
　athletic growths, 81-82
　awesomidity, 73, 75
　character growths, 75-78
　personal growths, 78-81
　results of, 7
　structure, diagram, 74
Guenther, Sue, xi

H

Hagstrom, W.O., 85
Hale, Bruce K., 32
Hastad, D.N., 86
Hoover, Thomas, 85

J

Jampolsky, Gerald G., 85
Johnson, Spencer, 85

K

Klopp, Audrey, xi

L

Lao-Tzu, 75
Larson, C.E., 85
Lawther, John, 85
Left brain dominance

changing to right brain, 12
characteristics of, 10
functions of, 10
illustration, 13

M

Martina, Joe, xi
Martins, R., 86
Matthews, Jack, 85
Meyer, Christa, xi
Meyer, June E., ii, iii, ix, vii
Meyer, Ray, vii, xv
Meyer, Rob, xi
Meyer, Suzi, xi
Mortensen, C. David, 86

N

Null, Marie, xi

P

Patent, Arnold M., 86
Penman, K.A., 86
Peterson, J., 86
Petrillo, Larry, xi
Plodzien, Carol A., ii, iii, iv, vii

R

Right brain dominance
  changing from left brain to, 12
  characteristics, 10-11
  functions of, 10
  illustration, 13
Risk
  awareness of, 66
  cause of regression, 68
  defining of for self, 66-68
  definition of, 66
  experiencing success, 70
  overcoming fears of failure, 66, 70
    illustrations, 69, 70
    use visual imagery, 70
  self-belief, 65-66
  structure of, 64
  use of xiv, 7
  wall of frustrations, 68-69
    illustration, 68

S

Self-belief, advantages of, xiv
Self-talk
  analysis of, 31
  negative, 31, 32-36
    examples, 33, 34, 35
    key words, 33
  positive, 32, 36
    key words, 36
  speed of, 31
Selvin, H.C., 85
Shakespeare, William, 33
Sherrod, Barbara, 10, 11, 86
Smith, R.E., 86
Smoll, F.L., 86

T

Thiel, William, xi
Thinking straight
  advantages use of, ix, xiv, 79, 80
  athletic growths, 81-82
    experiences, 81-82
  awareness human mind (*see* Brain functions)
  characters of (*see* Characters of thinking straight)
  concepts of, 7
  definition, 7
  end result of, 75
  goal of, 11, 12-13
  goals of athletes (*see* Goals)
  keys to, 7
    communication (*see* Communication)
    diagram, 6
    goals (*see* Goals)
    growth (*see* Growth)
    risk (*see* Risk)
    work (*see* Work)
  making choices, xiii
  personal growth of athletes, 78-81
  positive experiences of athletes, 79
  risk taking (*see* Risk)
  self-belief (*see* Self-belief)
  use language of by teammates, 80-81

V

Van Sluys, Loralie, xi
Volberding, Joan, xi
Volleyball practice, sports dialogue, 38

W

Whitmont, Edward C., 86
Whole brain thinking, 11-13
  as goal of thinking straight, 11
  changing left to right brain, 12
  processes for, 11-12
  use of, 12-13
Wilson, Colin, 86
Work
  direct energy (*see* Conditioning)
  negative energy, 58
  physical work toward goal, 60-62
  practice self-discipline, 58-60
    negative energy, 58-59
    positive energy, 59
    rewards of, 59-60
    term defined, 58
  responsibility for, 55-56
  self output, 55-56
  set intentions, 56-58
    sequence for focusing mind, 57
  structure of, diagram, 54
  use of, 7

Z

Zdenek, Marilee, 10
Zelhard Jr., P.F., 85